The Evolution of U.S. Military Policy from the Constitution to the Present

Gian Gentile, Michael E. Linick, Michael Shurkin

Prepared for the United States Army
Approved for public release; distribution unlimited

For more information on this publication, visit www.rand.org/t/RR1759

Library of Congress Cataloging-in-Publication Data is available for this publication.
ISBN: 978-0-8330-9786-6

Published by the RAND Corporation, Santa Monica, Calif.
© Copyright 2017 RAND Corporation
RAND® is a registered trademark.

Support RAND
Make a tax-deductible charitable contribution at
www.rand.org/giving/contribute

www.rand.org

Preface

Since the earliest days of the Republic, American political and military leaders have debated and refined the national approach to providing an Army to win the nation's independence and provide for its defense against all enemies, foreign and domestic. Based on a larger RAND study of the history of U.S. military policy from the Constitution to the present, this report provides historical background to understand the evolution of the fundamental laws that have shaped the organization of the Army and its employment at home and overseas from the colonial era to the present day. Through archival research of primary sources and a survey of the historical literature, the report traces the evolution of U.S. military policy, highlighting the legal, political, and security compromises that contributed to a new interpretation of the Constitution's "raise and support armies" and "militia" clauses. These legal decisions were not natural or inevitable lines drawn directly from the Constitution to the present day. Rather, the Army of today and the laws that govern it were contingent on the resolution of broader political, cultural, and intellectual debates over the necessity of a standing professional force, the power of the federal government, and the principled obligation of citizens to their Nation.

This report explains the origins of today's Army and contributes to ongoing debates over how the nation should organize and employ its Army. This report should be of interest to force planners and anyone interested in the organization and employment of the Army's three components—the Regular Army, the Army National Guard, and the Army Reserve—and the evolution of military policy in American history.

This research was sponsored by Headquarters Department of the Army (HQDA) G8, Army Quadrennial Defense Review (QDR) Office, and conducted within the RAND Arroyo Center's Strategy, Doctrine, and Resources Program. RAND Arroyo Center, part of the RAND Corporation, is a federally funded research and development center sponsored by the United States Army. The analysis and primary evidence in this research report is based on a larger four-volume history of U.S. military policy from the Constitution to the present sponsored by HQDA G8, Army QDR Office. That larger four-volume history effort has an advisory board of six leading scholars of history, public policy, and constitutional law. They have provided scholarly feedback and criticism for each of the four volumes, and we have used their input in the writing of this research report.

The Project Unique Identification Code (PUIC) for the project that produced this document is RAN157253.

Contents

Summary

The laws that govern the U.S. Army have changed little since 1940. These laws have become so familiar that many assume they constitute a "traditional" U.S. military policy, emanating from the Constitution's division of federal and state powers. Drawing on a RAND study of the history of Army and the evolution of laws that authorize, empower, and govern it, in this report we show that the current set of foundational laws for the Army were not an inevitable interpretation of the "raise and support armies" or "militia" clauses of the Constitution. Rather, U.S. military policy has evolved over time through statutory changes. These laws emerged from long-standing debates over the role of civilian-soldiers, the necessity of a standing professional force (i.e., the Regular Army), the relationship between the Army and the potential sources of manpower for expansion, the balance of federal and state authorities, and the nation's security needs. A series of legislative compromises between 1903 and 1940 established a consensus that forms the foundation of current military policy. By highlighting the evolution of military policy, this history introduces new questions about the traditional nature of the Army that exists today and supplies a context for future efforts to rethink how the Army might continue to evolve to meet the nation's changing security needs.

Acknowledgments

Throughout the project, our sponsor, Timothy Muchmore of Army G-8 Quadrennial Defense Review Office, provided very valuable input with drafts and a deep commitment to this history of U.S. military policy, for which the RAND team is very thankful and deeply indebted. Sally Sleeper, director of the RAND Arroyo Strategy, Doctrine, and Resources Program, provided us with encouragement and sound advice along the way. We are indebted to RAND Arroyo director Tim Bonds for providing some additional assistance at a crucial point in the archival research process. Special thanks go to Paul Steinberg of RAND for his expert work in helping us first write and then polish this report in its final form. We owe a lot to the four reviewers of this report: Jerry Cooper, professor emeritus at the University of Missouri–St. Louis; Joshua Klimas of RAND; Stephen Vladeck, professor of constitutional law at the University of Texas at Austin; and Tom McNaugher, former RAND Arroyo director. We also are indebted to two additional helpful reviews by Professor Brian Linn of Texas A&M University and by Lieutenant Colonel Jason Warren of the U.S. Army War College. As mentioned in the preceding summary, we used the criticism and input of our six Advisory Board members for the larger four-volume work: Professor Beth Bailey of Kansas University; Brigadier General (retired) Lance Betros; Rob Citino, senior historian at the National World War II Museum; Brigadier General (retired) Robert Doughty; Tom McNaugher, former RAND Arroyo director; and Professor Stephen Vladeck of the University of Texas at Austin. Many thanks also go to Tamara Elliot of the U.S. Senate Library, who was always there for help in acquiring primary documents and for providing expertise on American legislative history. Anne Armstrong and Ryan Trainor at the National Guard Museum provided the research team with access to a trove of primary evidence. At the Hagley Museum and Library, we appreciate the assistance of Roger Horowitz and Lucas R. Clawson. Gail Kouril and Betsy Hammes, both senior librarians at RAND, provided very helpful assistance and suggestions for the research done on this project. We want to thank the RAND team on the larger four-volume history for their research assistance and helpful criticisms of this draft: Badreddine Ahtchi, Alexandra Evans, Adam Givens, Jameson Karns, Wade Markel, Miranda Priebe, Sarah Soliman, Elizabeth Tencza, and Sean Zeigler. Lastly, we thank RAND's James Torr for his expert editing and Todd Duft, Marcy Agmon, Martha Friese, Jessica Bateman, Yamit Feinberg, Patrice Lester, and Lisa Sodders for shepherding this report through the publication process.

CHAPTER ONE

Introduction

The current institutional arrangement of the Army, which comprises a Regular Army and two reserve components (RCs)—the Army National Guard of the United States (ARNGUS) and the U.S. Army Reserve (USAR)—has the look and feel of something necessary and inevitable. As a result, when debating the Army's size, appropriate roles and functions, and the laws required to authorize, empower, and govern the Army, it is easier to think about evolving institutional modifications rather than to question the underlying assumptions and prevailing paradigms or to propose fundamental changes to the statutory organization of the Army. Looking to history, in this report we argue that, on the contrary, there is little about the Army's organization that is inevitable or necessary, a fact that should give policymakers license to explore a wider range of options for the Army of the future.[1]

The National Commission on the Future of the Army (NCFA), which Congress established as part of the National Defense Authorization Act of 2015, is a case in point. Congress gave the NCFA the mandate to, among other things, examine the

---

[1] Prominent American military historical surveys are Emory Upton, *The Military Policy of the United States*, 4th ed., Washington, D.C.: U.S. Government Printing Office, (1903) 1917; William Winthrop, *Military Law and Precedents*, Boston: Little, Brown, and Company, 1896; Marvin A. Kreidberg and Merton G. Henry, *History of Military Mobilization in the United States Army, 1775–1945*, Washington, D.C.: Department of the Army, 1955; Richard H. Kohn, *Eagle and Sword: Federalists and the Creation of the Military Establishment in America, 1783–1802*, New York: Free Press, 1975; Allan R. Millett, Peter Maslowski, and William B. Feis, *For the Common Defense: A Military History of the United States from 1607–2012*, New York: Free Press, 2012; I. B. Holley and John McAuley Palmer, *General John M. Palmer, Citizen Soldiers, and the Army of a Democracy*, Westport, Conn.: Greenwood Press, 1982; Eilene Marie Slack Galloway, *History of United States Military Policy on Reserve Forces, 1775–1957*, Washington, D.C.: U.S. Government Printing Office, 1957; Russell Frank Weigley, *Towards an American Army: Military Thought from Washington to Marshall*, New York: Columbia University Press, 1962; Russell Frank Weigley, *History of the United States Army*, New York: Macmillan, 1967; Russell Frank Weigley, *The American Way of War: A History of United States Military Strategy and Policy*, New York: Macmillan, 1973; U.S. House of Representatives, *Review of the Reserve Program: Hearing Before the Subcommittee No. 1 of the Committee on Armed Services*, Washington, D.C., Government Printing Office, February 4–8, 18–21, 1957. A reference guide for the legislation behind the military policy can be found in Richard H. Kohn, *The United States Military Under the Constitution of the United States, 1789–1989*, New York: New York University Press, 1991.

assumptions behind the Army's current size and force mixture.[2] Despite its mandate, the NCFA elected not to reconsider the Army's statutory authorities and responsibilities and instead focused on ways to refine and improve the force that exists. For example, the commission's published report cites the phrase "traditional military policy of the United States," quoted verbatim from the current set of federal laws that govern the Army and national defense. By using this phrasing, the NCFA reinforces the idea that a coherent and constant "traditional military policy" has governed the Army from the earliest days of the Republic. The NCFA's report offers 63 recommendations for such things as improving Army training and readiness, adjusting organizational structures, rebalancing the Regular Army and the Army's two reserve components, and improving personnel management. Yet none of the 63 recommendations calls for a reconsideration of the fundamental laws that authorize, empower, and govern the Army. The nation has "one Army" and a "traditional military policy," notes the NCFA report, for sound "historical, cultural, legal, operational, and strategic" reasons.[3]

The notion of a coherent and constant *traditional* military policy stretching from the earliest days of the Republic to today is, however, a myth. Indeed, the term *military policy* was not used in the United States until the decades following the end of the American Civil War, when Colonel Emory Upton, a highly decorated Army officer and influential reformer, first coined it in the title of his groundbreaking work, *The Military Policy of the United States*. (As used by Upton, the term *military policy* connoted matters pertaining to the U.S. Army, such as the laws that govern the institution and the policies for wartime expansion, and today the term continues to refer to Army matters to the exclusion of the other services.)

We highlight the etymology of the term to underline the fact that today's military policy is not the result of a coherent tradition but rather the aggregate of over two centuries of disagreements and compromises between various competing interests and ideas, many of which reflected the political and cultural debates of the day and the need to meet the military requirements of the nation's security of the time. For each generation since the Constitutional Framers, ideology, political culture, and institutional momentum have limited the discourse on military policy and constrained the range of options available for serious consideration.

Indeed, the current force structure is strikingly different from anything the Framers of the Constitution imagined. Once considered anathema, the United States now largely entrusts its national security to a standing, professional force—its Regular Army. To augment its regular forces, the Army also maintains two professionalized standing reserve components that are resourced and organized under the "raise and support armies" clause of the Constitution. Once organized to defend a growing

---

[2] National Commission on the Future of the Army, *Report to the President and to Congress*, Arlington, Va., January 28, 2016.

[3] National Commission on the Future of the Army, 2016, p. 1.

nation protected by two oceans, the Army can now deploy globally and fight decisively on very short notice. Along these lines, we argue that the relative influence of two constitutional clauses—the armies clause and the militia clause—has evolved as the nation has grown and as its dynamic security needs have changed. Over time, Congress's use of the armies clause to organize, train, equip, mobilize (call forth militias or order reserve components to active service), and expand (increase the overall size of the Army) the Army has increased in importance alongside a concomitant decline in the importance of the militia clause, which no longer serves as a principal statutory foundation for how Congress organizes and equips the Army.

The term *traditional military policy* first appeared in federal law in 1940, 60 years after Upton coined the phrase and it entered widespread use in American military and policy circles. As institutionalized in the U.S. Code, the term reflects a series of important legislative reforms between 1903 and 1940 that sought to adapt the laws that authorized, empowered, and governed the Army. We argue that the current set of fundamental federal laws written during this period have not changed measurably since. For example, Title 10, Subtitle B of the U.S. Code, which governs the Army, states that the Army consists of "the Regular Army, the Army National Guard of the United States, the Army National Guard while in the service of the United States, and the Army Reserve."[4] We argue that these foundational laws have remained virtually unchanged since 1940, despite significant changes in the geostrategic environment and the nation's increasing global interests and commitments. It is important to note that the laws passed between 1903 and 1940 reflect the debates and challenges of a particular historical period that differs greatly from the security environment that the nation confronts today. Figure 1.1 depicts the evolution of U.S. military policy across a timeline from 1775 to present. Along the top of the figure, we provide the strategic context across five periods—emerging America, the Civil War and the war with Spain, the World Wars, limited wars, and the Global War on Terror (GWOT)—as well as the size of the Army in those periods. Along the bottom of the timeline, we highlight the specific historical context in those periods, including the major wars fought and the size of the Army as it evolved over time in terms of the number of soldiers (the left axis) and the number of divisions (the right axis). In the middle of the timeline, we highlight the major relevant pieces of legislation that affected the evolution of the Army. The clear message of the figure is the absence of significant statutory change after 1940, something that is highlighted by the thick red lines and arrows in the middle of the figure.

In this report, we seek to correct popular misconceptions about the history of U.S. military policy and establish an authoritative foundation for the debate over the best design for the future Army force. Through archival research of primary sources and a survey of the historical literature, we examine the principal strategic assumptions underlying the current force and trace the emergence of the laws that govern the

---

[4] U.S. Code, Title 10, Subtitle B, Section 3062(c), Policy; Composition; Organized Peace Establishment, 2012.

Figure 1.1
The Evolution of U.S. Military Policy, 1775–Present

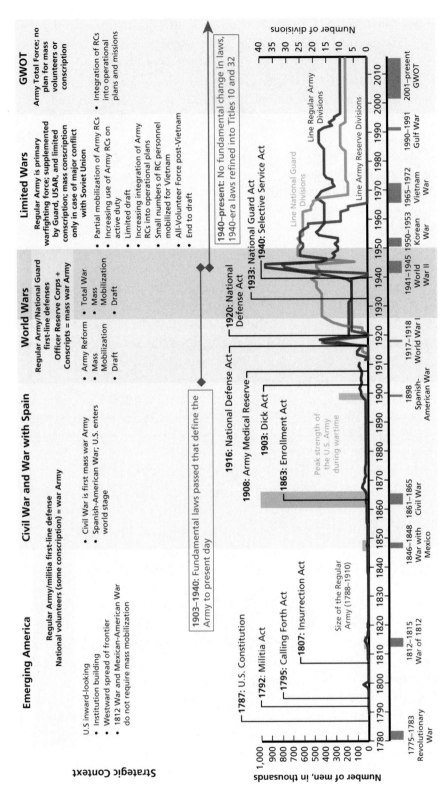

RAND RR1759-1.1

Army today. The following history has policy relevance because it shows that change in military policy is both possible and necessary. When senior political and military leaders design Army force structure, they should not permit their thinking to be constrained by such historically loaded terms as *traditional military policy*. When imagining a future force, senior political and military leaders should recognize that current statutory foundations could be further refined to enhance the Army's ability to meet the nation's dynamic security needs.

The remainder of this report traces the history through four periods: origins, the 19th century system, from the Spanish-American War to total war, and from the Korean War to total force policy. We end with some broader conclusions. We also provide an annex that shows in tabular form the history of legislation pertaining to the evolution of U.S. military policy.

CHAPTER TWO

The Constitutional Moorings for the Evolution of U.S. Military Policy

The legal foundation for the U.S. Army can be found in the Constitution. More specifically, Article 1, Section 8, includes the "raise and support armies" clause, which empowers Congress to create and support an army of undetermined size and composition. It also includes the militia clause, which gives Congress the power to "provide for calling forth the Militia to execute the Laws of the Union, suppress Insurrections and repel invasions" and for Congress to "provide for organizing, arming, and disciplining the militia, and for governing such part of them as may be employed in the service of the United States, reserving to the States respectively, the appointment of the officers, and the authority of training the militia according to the discipline provided by Congress." In addition, Article 2, Section 2, names the President the "Commander and Chief" of the Army, the Navy, and "the Militia of the several States, when called into the actual Service of the United States." In the early years of the Republic and into the 19th century, Congress used these clauses as a constitutional basis for an Army that consisted of two distinct elements: (1) a small professional standing army of regulars, to be used principally on the frontier to defend sites of strategic significance and in assisting the spread of wester settlers, and in case of an invasion by an external power, and (2) local militias to be used primarily to suppress civil unrest and enforce state and national laws but also to provide forces to repel invasions.[1]

This basic formula was not immediately conceived during the Constitutional Convention but reflected the Framers' assumptions, experiences, ideological convictions, and political compromises. The colonial militia, for example, was not the most effective instrument of collective security available—although some at the time did believe that to be the case—but rather what 18th century Americans knew and had

---

[1] For a recent and excellent analysis of the original understanding toward executive power in the Constitution, see Saikrishna Bangalore Prakash, *Imperial from the Beginning: The Constitution of the Original Executive*, New Haven, Conn.: Yale University Press, 2015. See also Jack N. Rakove, *Original Meanings: Politics and Ideas in the Making of the Constitution*, New York: Vintage Books, 1997; Gordon S. Wood, *The Creation of the American Republic, 1776–1787*, Chapel Hill, N.C.: University of North Carolina Press, 1998; Don Higginbotham, "The Federalized Militia Debate: A Neglected Aspect of Second Amendment Scholarship," *The William and Mary Quarterly*, Vol. 55, No. 1, January 1998.

relied on for local protection since the earliest days of colonization and for centuries prior in England. Similarly, 18th century Americans, owing to an ideology and political culture forged through colonial experience and popular interpretations of the English Civil War, viewed a strong standing army in the hands of a sovereign power as a potential threat to liberty. Local militias were generally capable of defending against the Native American threat and were typically loyal to the communities from which they came; virtually all adult white men were subject to compulsory militia service, although some did volunteer for duty.[2] Each member of a local militia was responsible for equipping himself and normally received no militia pay, and the ability of the colonies to pay for military capabilities beyond this was highly limited. Americans of the era were also disinclined to pay for a military capability when a large ocean protected them from aggressive external enemies.

Imperial war reinforced American antipathy toward standing armies. Colonial British governors pushed colonists to maintain militia companies to defend against potential invasion by foreign powers. During the Seven Years' War (1756–1763), colo-

---

[2] See Bernard Bailyn's seminal classic, *The Ideological Origins of the American Revolution*, Cambridge, Mass.: Belknap Press, 1967. On the colonial militia, see Ian Beckett, *Britain's Part-Time Soldiers: The Amateur Military Tradition, 1558–1945*, Barnsley, UK: Pen & Sword, 2011; Frederick T. Wilson and U.S. Adjutant-General's Office, *Federal Aid in Domestic Disturbances, 1787–1903*, Washington, D.C.: U.S. Government Printing Office, 1903; Richard H. Kohn, "The Murder of the Militia System in the Aftermath of the American Revolution," in Stanley J. Underdal, ed., *Military History of the American Revolution: The Proceedings of the 6th Military History Symposium United States Air Force Academy 10–11 October 1974*, Washington, D.C.: U.S. Government Printing Office, 1976; Jason W. Warren, *Connecticut Unscathed: Victory in the Great Narragansett War, 1675–1676*, Norman, Okla.: University of Oklahoma Press, 2014; Kyle F. Zelner, *A Rabble in Arms: Massachusetts Towns and Militiamen During King Philip's War*, New York: New York University Press, 2010; John Grenier, *The First Way of War: American War Making on the Frontier, 1607–1814*, Cambridge, UK: Cambridge University Press, 2005; Wayne E. Lee, *Barbarians and Brothers: Anglo-American Warfare, 1500–1865*, Oxford, UK: Oxford University Press, 2011; Richard Henry Marcus, *The Militia of Colonial Connecticut, 1639–1775*, PhD dissertation, Boulder, Colo.: University of Colorado, 1965; Jonathan Smith, "How Massachusetts Raised Her Troops in the American Revolution," *Massachusetts Historical Society*, 1922; Ira Gruber, "The Anglo-American Military Tradition and the War for American Independence," in Kenneth J. Hagan and William R. Roberts, eds., *Against All Enemies: Interpretations of American Military History from Colonial Times to the Present*, Westport, Conn.: Greenwood Press, 1986; Charles Royster, *A Revolutionary People at War: The Continental Army and American Character, 1775–1783*, Chapel Hill, N.C.: University of North Carolina Press, 1979; John Shy, *A People Numerous and Armed: Reflections on the Military Struggle for American Independence*, Oxford, UK: Oxford University Press, 1976; Don Higginbotham, *The War of American Independence; Military Attitudes, Policies, and Practice, 1763–1789*, New York: Macmillan, 1971; "The Debate Over National Military Institutions: An Issue Slowly Resolved, 1775–1815," in William M. Fowler, Jr., and Wallace Coyle, eds., *The American Revolution: Changing Perspectives*, Boston: Northeastern, 1979; Mark Edward Lender, "The Social Structure of the New Jersey Brigade: The Continental Line as an American Standing Army," in Peter Karsten, ed., *The Military in America: From the Colonial Era to the Present*, New York: Free Press, 1980; Arthur A. Ekirch, Jr., *The Civilian and the Military: A History of the American Anti-Militarist Tradition*, Oakland, Calif.: Independent Institute, 2010; Steven J. Rosswurm, *Arms, Country, and Class: The Philadelphia Militia and the Lower Sort During the American Revolution*, New Brunswick, N.J.: Rutgers University Press, 1989. The most thorough coverage of the historiography of the American militia and National Guard, which by its topical nature also addresses military policy, is Jerry Cooper, *The Militia and National Guard in America Since Colonial Times: A Reference Guide*, Westport, Conn.: Greenwood Press, 1993.

nial militias often augmented British forces against the French and their Indian allies. Colonists chafed under the rigors and harshness of life in a professional military, leading many colonists to see the empire and its representatives as external threats to their own liberty and interests.[3] The British leadership's low opinion of the local militias was partially the result of a lack of continuous training and militiamen's inability to serve for extended periods because of their simultaneous business, work, and familial responsibilities.[4] After the war's end, from about 1761 to 1776, a series of uprisings and violent protests against British taxation increased tensions within the colonies. The presence of British regulars sent to enforce the taxes bolstered the spreading belief among colonists that a standing army in the hands of the monarch was a threat to freedom.

The Revolutionary War forced a shift away from the American reliance on local militias alone. In June 1775, the Continental Congress formed a regular army, known as the Continental Army. Individual states used their ability to draft men for both local militia units and to meet quotas to fill the new army's ranks. Recruitment and supply issues remained, but the militias' unpredictability during battle remained an intractable problem during the war and an enduring memory for many in positions of political authority thereafter. Despite their shortcomings, however, militiamen were an invaluable police force, because they kept state governments out of Loyalist control and ensured adherence to the cause.[5] Combinations of militias and regular forces won some of the most important American battlefield victories against the British Army. Famously, at the Battle of Cowpens in South Carolina in 1781, the Americans used the militias' poor reputation to lure the British into a deadly double envelopment. Successes and failures of both the Continental Army and the militias acted as the catalyst for a significant debate after the war over whether the young Republic's national defense should be premised on the militias, a standing army, or some combination of the two.[6]

There was no consensus about what the Army of the new Republic should be. The Framers of the Constitution disagreed over whether there should be a Regular Army at all and, if one were to be established, over both the relative roles of the Regular Army and militias and the relationship between the federal government and the militias. Federalists such as Alexander Hamilton, Henry Knox, and, most important, George Washington—who detailed his vision for the Army in his 1783 pamphlet *Sentiments*

---

[3] Fred Anderson, *Crucible of War: The Seven Years' War and the Fate of Empire in British North America, 1754–1766*, New York: Alfred A. Knopf, 2000, p. 167.

[4] John Shy, "A New Look at the Colonial Militia," *William and Mary Quarterly*, Vol. 3, No. 20, 1963; Fred Anderson, *A People's Army: Massachusetts Soldiers and Society in the Seven Years' War*, Chapel Hill, N.C.: University of North Carolina Press, 1984.

[5] Matthew C. Ward, "The American Militias: 'The Garnish of the Table'?" in Roger Chicerking and Stig Förster, ed., *War in an Age of Revolution, 1775–1815*, Cambridge, UK: Cambridge University Press, 2010.

[6] Smith, 1922; Gruber, 1986; Royster, 1979; Shy, 1976; Higginbotham, 1971; "The Debate Over National Military Institutions: An Issue Slowly Resolved, 1775–1815," 1979; Lender, 1980.

on a Peace Establishment—were skeptical of the value of poorly trained or prepared militias.[7] Yet they did not argue for a large professional standing army because they understood their fellow compatriots' fears and the fiscal demands such a force would place on the new nation. The Framers were searching for an alternative to the large and expensive standing armies in European countries at the time. Their solution was to form a small national professional army backed by a standardized federalized militia— "almost an Army reserve" or "national militia."[8] The Framers insisted that the militias be "regulated," meaning that the legislative branch was to ensure that the militias were equipped and trained to a certain standard, perhaps by designating a "select militia" to serve under federal control as part of the Regular Army for use when needed, before transitioning to full state control.

In contrast, critics of the Constitution, such as Elbridge Gerry and Luther Martin, had a higher regard for the militia. Chiefly for political and cultural reasons, they believed that the country had to entrust its defense to civilian soldiers rather than professionals in a standing force and thus sought to place the entire burden of national defense on the militias of the several states. They were hostile to proposals for any standing army and opposed giving the federal government a strong hand in the state militia systems. For the critics of the Constitution, the state militias were the Army, not a reserve; if there were to be a standing Regular Army, it was to be kept exceedingly small, with a minimalist mission to guard stores and arsenals and, when necessary, defend against Native Americans.[9]

The debate between Federalists and Constitutional critics on military policy formed a basis for a set of competing ideas about what the Army should be: the "professionalist" mindset and the "militia" mindset.[10] Again, no one argued for a large

---

[7] Ward, 2010; George Washington, "Sentiments on a Peace Establishment, 1783," in Henry C. Dethloff and Gerald E. Shenk, eds., *Citizen and Soldier: A Sourcebook on Military Service and National Defense from Colonial America to the Present*, New York and London: Routledge, (1783) 2011.

[8] Quotes are from Kohn, 1975, p. 88. See also Washington, (1783) 2011, p. 22; F. W. von Steuben, "A Letter on the Subject of an Established Militia," New York, 1784; Alexander Hamilton, *Continental Congress Report on a Military Establishment*, Washington, D.C., June 18, 1783; George Washington, "Letter to Baron von Steuben," Mount Vernon, March 15, 1784.

[9] James Brown Scott, *The Militia: Extracts from the Journals and Debates of the Federal Convention, the State Constitutional Conventions, the Congress, the Federalist, Together with Papers Relating to the Militia of the United States*, 64th Congress, 2d Session, Senate, Document No. 695, January 12, 1917.

[10] Although both of Russell Weigley's books, *History of the United States Army* and *Towards an American Army*, contain some problematic interpretations, their intellectual history of the U.S. Army and characterization of the Army's intellectual environment still make them useful for understanding the history of American military policy. We also rely on other important works that cover the history of the U.S. Army and American military policy, namely Brian Linn's review essay "The American Way of War Revisited," *The Journal of Military History*, Vol. 66, April 2002. Also see Linn's excellent *The Echo of Battle: The Army's Way of War*, Cambridge, Mass.: Harvard University Press, 2010; Millett, Maslowski, and Feis, 2012; Antulio J. Echevarria, *Reconsidering the American Way of War: U.S. Military Practice from the Revolution to Afghanistan*, Washington, D.C.: Georgetown University Press, 2014.

standing force, but "professionalists" such as Washington were more favorably disposed toward the Regular Army and were interested in ensuring the professional qualities of both the Regular Army and the militias. This school thought the Regular Army to be an effective fighting force and sought to guarantee the quality of the militias by providing for their organization and discipline rather than relying on poorly trained and prepared military amateurs to fight on relatively short notice. Proponents of the militia school, in contrast, tended to be more positive in their assessment of both militias and citizens' capacity to be turned into part-time soldiers in time to appropriately address emerging threats and stressed the militias' primacy within the American security system.[11]

This intellectual debate that began with the Constitution continues to shape and inform the evolution of military policy up to the present day. Importantly, the militia mindset drew on two related traditions in American society:

1.   a compulsory militia tradition, which required all adult white males to serve in state-organized militia units, although it never really functioned as intended

2.   a volunteer militia tradition made up of men who, on their own volition, organized volunteer militia units without being directed to do so by state governments.[12]

Thus, four central elements—(1) the intellectual debate between the professionalist and militia mindsets, (2) the compulsory and volunteer militia traditions, (3) the militia and armies clauses of the Constitution, and (4) the laws passed by Congress to govern the Army—combined with changes in the larger strategic context and the character of warfare to shape the development of U.S military policy from 1788 to 1940.

Taken as a whole, the post-1788 changes to the Army unfold within two historical periods. The first period ran from 1792 to 1898, when Congress passed a series of laws

---

[11] For a recently published excellent revisionist history of the ratification debates, see Pauline Maier, *Ratification: The People Debate the Constitution, 1787–1788*, New York: Simon and Schuster, 2011; Anonymous, "The Federalist Farmer No. XVIII," in Herbert J. Storing, ed., *The Complete Anti-Federalist*, Chicago: University of Chicago Press, 1788. Also see David P. Currie, *The Constitution in Congress: The Federalist Period, 1789–1801*, Chicago: University of Chicago Press, 1999, pp. 84–88; Rakove, 1997; Willi Paul Adams, *The First American Constitutions: Republican Ideology and the Making of the State Constitutions in the Revolutionary Era*, Lanham, Md.: Rowman & Littlefield Publishers, 2001.

[12] Jerry M. Cooper, *The Rise of the National Guard: The Evolution of the American Militia, 1865–1920*, Lincoln: University of Nebraska Press, 1998; John K. Mahon, *History of the Militia and the National Guard*, New York; London: Collier Macmillan, 1983, pp. 110–111; Joseph John Holmes, *The National Guard of Pennsylvania: Policeman of Industry, 1865–1905*, PhD dissertation, Storrs, Conn.: University of Connecticut, 1971; Henry Martyn Boies, "Our National Guard," *Harper's New Monthly Magazine*, 1880; "A Brief History of the Oldest Minnesota National Guard Company," *National Guardsman*, May 1901; Martha Derthick, *The National Guard in Politics*, Cambridge, Mass.: Harvard University Press, 1965; Michael D. Doubler, *I Am the Guard: A History of the Army National Guard, 1636–2000*, Washington, D.C.: Army National Guard, 2001; Raymond F. Pisney, *The Brandywine Rangers in the War of 1812*, Wilmington, Del.: Hagley Museum & Library, 1950.

that transformed the local militias into something significantly different from what was first envisioned by the Framers of the Constitution. To a large degree, the changes reflected efforts to address the inadequacies of the constitutional basis for the Army that made it difficult for the nation to rapidly mobilize forces adequate in number and quality for the challenges facing the young nation. These challenges included internal insurrection, with early examples being Shay's Rebellion (1786–1787), the Whiskey Rebellion (1791–1794), and the Indian Wars, which stretched from the earliest years of the Republic to late in the 19th century. In addition, the United States fought major wars during this era: the War of 1812, the Mexican-American War (1846–1848), the Civil War (1861–1865), and the Spanish-American War (1898). Notably, this period saw a gradual but significant change in U.S. military policy that reflected the increasing size and complexity of America's wars. The period also witnessed the increasing importance of the Constitution's "raise and support armies" clause in organizing, training, equipping, mobilizing, and expanding the size of the Army and the declining role of the militia clause.

The second period began after the Spanish-American War, a watershed moment for American military policy because of the reforms inspired by the American military's poor performance in the war and the significantly greater requirements resulting from the United States' new position as a world power. Between 1898 and 1940, Congress passed a series of laws that gave shape to the legislative framework that governs today's Army.[13] Between 1903 and 1940, policymakers sought to address the inadequacies of the ad hoc methods used for Army expansion that were revealed by the Spanish-American War and subsequent conflicts in Europe. To strengthen the military, Congress had to address the widening gap between the capabilities the nation required and those that were in place at the start of the 20th century and adapt to profound changes in the strategic context and the character of warfare. The primary force for change for this period was the growing premium placed on preparedness—the need for ready forces to defend overseas possessions and the need for larger, more capable, and more readily available land armies in an era of industrial warfare.[14]

---

[13] See the annex for a chart that lays out in detail the major statutory laws and their evolution from 1787 to 1940.

[14] Of course, the period from 1940 up to the present witnessed many changes both in how America fought its wars and in the greater strategic environment. However, after 1940, there were no fundamental alterations to the foundational laws—military policy—that govern the U.S. Army. Instead, the focus during these years was on the methods for mobilization and Army expansion and the proper force mix and allocation of resources between the Army's three components. We address this period in Chapter Five.

CHAPTER THREE

The 19th Century System

One of the chief features of the evolution in military policy after 1788 was the rapid re-interpretation of the Constitution's Article 1, Section 8 (militia clause), and Article 2, Section 2 (commander-in-chief clause), through a new series of statutes that redefined the roles of the Regular Army and the militias and recalibrated the relationship between the militias, Congress, and the President. In only 20 years, Congress forged a markedly different militia from that envisioned by the Framers to adapt the Army to the nation's changing security needs.

Initially, the nascent Republic struggled to maintain even the smallest Regular Army and could barely cope with threats posed by Native Americans and internal rebellions, let alone the risk of invasion by foreign powers. The Regular Army had a meager strength of 800 soldiers and relied on local militias produced by the states to expand when needed. However, both the Regular Army and the militias were critically under-resourced, with the end result of a force incapable of conducting effective operations on the frontier. This point was brought home in 1791 when Native American tribes decisively defeated a combined force of roughly 1,100 Regular Army troops and levies and 300 militiamen during a series of deadly engagements known as the Battle of the Wabash in the Northwestern Territory of Ohio. In the last of these deadly clashes, the militiamen, who were isolated from the larger force, were attacked, causing the majority of them to flee and leading to the virtual annihilation of the remaining regular troops.[1]

President George Washington and his advisors, foremost among them Secretary of War Henry Knox, pushed for legislation to ensure that the state militias would be available when needed to increase the size of the Army. They hoped to, at a minimum, establish a "well-regulated" compulsory militia in which nearly all adult white males were required to serve.[2] But rather than making the federal government responsible for the militias, as the Washington administration hoped, the result was "An Act to

---

[1] Kohn, 1975, pp. 115–116.

[2] Henry Knox, *A Plan for the General Arrangement of the Militia of the United States*, New York, March 28, 1786, pp. 28–36. Knox's plan that drew on previous proposals by Washington, Alexander Hamilton, and General Friedrich Wilhelm von Steuben.

More Effectually Provide for the National Defense by Establishing a Uniform Militia Throughout the United States" (known simply as the Uniform Militia Act of 1792), which afforded the states responsibility for organizing, training, and supplying militia units but provided no federal enforcing mechanisms.[3] From the Federalist perspective, the Militia Act had another significant shortcoming: It did not link the militias to the Regular Army and did not address the militias' role as a federal reserve force. The act did stipulate that militia service was compulsory for all free, able-bodied adult white males age 18–45, thus creating a large manpower pool for the states to draw on when organizing militia units. However, its directives on equipping, organizing, and training the state militias were more aspirational than binding, because the act did not provide mechanisms to force state compliance. In effect, the 1792 Militia Act failed to establish a statutory definition of the relationship between the Regular Army and the militias and the ways in which the militias would be used to increase the overall size of the Army. In other words, it did not establish a coherent, comprehensible, and enforceable military policy for the United States.

Congressional debates over the Militia Act provide insights into why the final act was very different from what Washington and Knox had envisioned. One of the central points of contention, as it was during the Constitutional Convention debates, was where power should lie with regard to both organizing, equipping, and training the States' militias and the authority to call them forth. Representative Jonathan Sturges of Connecticut reportedly argued that the power to train, equip, and determine exemptions from militia service rested with the states and that Congress should have the authority only to "organize" the militias when first called forward for service. In response, another congressman, clearly of the Federalist persuasion, noted that the "consequence" of Sturges' "motion would be, to render the power of Congress in organizing, arming and disciplining the militia, entirely nugatory." Although Federalist arguments like these were made, it was clear that the majority of Congress favored a defanged Knox Bill, which ultimately came to be the final Militia Act. Representative Abraham Clark of New Jersey noted facetiously that if Congress were given the centralizing authorities over the militia, as the Knox Bill proposed, then if "an old woman was to strike an excise officer with a broomstick, forsooth the military is to be called out to suppress an insurgency."[4]

---

[3] U.S. Statutes at Large, An Act to More Effectually to Provide for the National Defense by Establishing a Uniform Militia Throughout the United States, Second Congress, Session I, Chapter 33, May 8, 1792 (1 Stat. 271); Kohn, 1975, p. 137. The best history of the militia and military policy during the 1790s is John K. Mahon, *The Citizen Soldier in National Defense, 1789–1815*, PhD dissertation, Los Angeles: University of California at Los Angeles, 1950. See also John K. Mahon, "A Board of Officers Considers the Condition of the Militia in 1826," *Military Affairs*, Vol. 15, No. 2, 1951; John K. Mahon, *History of the Second Seminole War, 1835–1842*, Gainesville, Fla.: University Press of Florida, 1985; Robert Mahon, *The American Militia: Decade of Decision, 1789–1800*, Gainesville, Fla.: University Press of Florida, 1960.

[4] Annals of Congress, Houses of Representatives, 2nd Congress, 2nd Session, April 1792, p. 575.

At the same time that members of Congress debated the Militia Act, they also deliberated over what would become known as the "Calling Forth Act." On May 2, 1792—six days before passage of the Militia Act—Congress passed another act pertaining to militias. Whereas the Constitution gave *only Congress* the authority to "provide for calling forth the militia," the new law provided the President with the authority to call forth the militia of the several states to suppress insurrections, repel invasions, and enforce the laws of the land. However, Congress placed certain restrictions on the President, including the requirement that he receive an antecedent court order from a local magistrate or state official inviting the President to call forth the militias to deal with problems inside a state or a group of states that local governmental power could not manage.[5] During this period, Congress was only seasonally in session, and the judicial certificate created an avenue for the executive powers to utilize the militia while Congress was not in session. In other words, the President did not enjoy the independent authority to call forth the militias; he could act only in response to a request by local officials. Nonetheless, this Calling Forth Act was a significant departure from the militia envisioned by the Constitution, because the Framers' debates showed that Congress, and not the President, was to be the branch of the federal government that would have sole authority for "calling forth the militia."

Unsatisfied by the Calling Forth Act's provisions, some continued to agitate for reform. In March 1794, Congress debated proposals to authorize the President to raise 10,000 regular forces and to order the states to organize and hold in readiness the militia. Neither gained traction. As the young Republic struggled to build a sustainable economy, strengthening the military establishment appeared, as one congressman noted at the time, to be "a very useless expense."[6]

However, the Whiskey Rebellion's turn toward insurrection in July 1794 drew attention back to the problem of the nation's ability to suppress internal rebellion and dissent. On August 7, Washington drew on the Calling Forth Act to mobilize 13,000 militiamen to quell the insurgency. The militia performed below expectations. Incidents of desertion and cowardice were widespread, leading Representative Samuel Smith of Maryland to complain that the militia "was totally useless for the professed purposes of the institution."[7] Congressional concern over the federal government's difficulty in responding to civil unrest, coupled with trust in George Washington and the calm, evenhanded manner by which he handled the insurgents, overcame initial fears

---

[5] U.S. Statutes at Large, An Act to Provide for Calling Forth the Militia to Execute the Laws of the Union, Suppress Insurrections and Repel Invasions, Second Congress, Session I, Chapter 28, May 2, 1792 (1 Stat. 264). Also see David E. Engdahl, "Soldiers, Riots, and Revolutions: The Law and History of Military Troops in Civil Disorders," *Iowa Law Review*, Vol. 57, No. 1, October 1971; Robert Coakley, *The Role of Federal Military Forces in Domestic Disorders, 1789–1878*, Washington, D.C.: U.S. Army Center of Military History, 1989.

[6] Representative John Smilie, quoted in Annals of Congress, House of Representatives, 3rd Congress, 1st Session, May 1794, p. 736.

[7] Annals of Congress, House of Representatives, 3rd Congress, 2nd Session, February 1795, p. 1214.

that strengthening the President's control over the militia might tip the fragile relationship between the federal government and the states.[8] As Representative Theodore Sedgwick of Massachusetts, an active voice for reform, noted, it now appeared "anti-Republican to attempt to narrow the powers of this Government over the militia."[9] In February 1795, Congress lifted some of the Calling Forth Act's restrictions and authorized the President to directly "call forth" the militias for the purpose of suppressing civil disturbances.

One of the implications of this change was a blurring of the division of labor between the state militias and the Regular Army. The Framers of the Constitution envisioned the state militias as the tool of choice for dealing with civil and domestic matter, and intended to reserve the Regular Army for service along the frontier and, in concert with mobilized local militias, for repelling an invasion by a major foreign power. Indeed, it was this combination of the Regular Army and the state militias that made up the nation's "first-line defenses," a term that would become popular in the latter part of the 19th century. By 1795, Congress appeared to be losing interest in this distinction, and indeed in 1799 Congress temporarily authorized President John Adams to use federal regulars whenever he called forth the militia to manage domestic problems and enforce the law. This expansion of presidential authority was made permanent in the Insurrection Act of 1807,[10] which effectively abandoned the Constitution's delineation of the circumstances in which the state militias or federal regulars could be used.[11]

Despite the President's newfound authority to call forth both the state militias and the Regular Army to manage internal instability and repel invasions, Congress did not define a formal, legal relationship between the militias and the Regular Army or a process to increase the size of the Army in time of war or crisis. As an illustration, consider the current foundational federal law that defines the Army and is mentioned in the introduction to this report. The current law states that the Army "consists of

---

[8] Colonel William L. Shaw, "The Interrelationship of the United States Army and the National Guard," *Military Law Review*, No. 39, January 1966, pp. 47–49; David J. Barron and Martin S. Ledermen, "The Commander in Chief at the Lowest Ebb: A Constitutional History," *Harvard Law Review*, Vol. 121, No. 4, February 2008, pp. 956–957, 961–964; Alan Hirsch, "The Militia Clauses of the Constitution and the National Guard," *University of Cincinnati Law Review*, No. 56, 1988, pp. 930–939; Michael Bahar, "The Presidential Intervention Principle: The Domestic Use of the Military and the Power of the Several States," *Harvard National Security Journal*, Vol. 5, No. 2, 2014, pp. 579–582.

[9] Annals of Congress, House of Representatives, 3rd Congress, 2nd Session, January 1795, p. 1069.

[10] U.S. Statutes at Large, An Act Authorizing the Employment of the Land and Naval Forces of the United States, in Case of Insurrections, Tenth Congress, Session II, Chapter 39, March 8, 1807 (2 Stat. 443); Robert Coakley, *Federal Use of Militia and the National Guard in Civil Disturbances*, Washington, D.C.: Brookings Institution, 1941; Bennett Milton Rich, *The Presidents and Civil Disorder*, Washington, D.C.: Brookings Institution, 1941; Frederick T. Wilson, *Federal Aid in Domestic Disturbances, 1787–1903*, New York: Arno Press, 1969.

[11] Stephen I. Vladeck, "Emergency Power and the Militia Acts," *The Yale Law Journal*, Vol. 114, No. 1, October 2004, pp. 157–161, 162–166.

the Regular Army, the Army National Guard of the United States, the Army National Guard while in the service of the United States, and the Army Reserve." During the early years of the Republic, there was no equivalent military policy or fundamental laws to define the relationship between the Army components. Hypothetically, it might have read something like "The Army of the United States consists of the Regular Army, the militias of the several states when called into federal service, and the national volunteers when war or emergency demands their calling." This is a fabrication; although there were certainly many federal laws written for the *Regular Army* and plenty of state laws for the *state militias*, no single federal law defined a *total army force* at that time. Accordingly, and unlike today, no federal enforcement mechanism existed to make the militias of the several states conform to the organization and discipline prescribed by Congress in the 1792 Militia Act. To offer an additional historical hypothetical fabrication, such a legal mechanism might have read as follows:

> For the militias of the several states to achieve the discipline and organization provided in this Act, Congress will allocate a total sum of 400,000 dollars a year to the state militias, distributed based on the number of men assigned on the muster roles of active militia units. State Adjutants General will provide yearly reports of the number of days of militia training per year, and Regular Army officers will inspect the militias to ensure their conformity to this Act. If the states are not in conformity to this Act, then their yearly authorization of funding will be withheld.

These hypothetical examples are intended to illustrate what a military policy *might* have looked like. But in the absence of such a functioning military policy, with laws to define the relationship between the Regular Army and the local militias, the federal government developed two mechanisms to expand the Army when needed. The federal government could request the states to provide either the *Common Militia* (also known as *Compulsory Militia*) and the *Volunteer Militia* for federal service.

Until the War of 1812, the federal government expanded the Army primarily through the states' Common Militia companies. The 1792 Militia Act was the federal authority to form compulsory militias along with states' laws authorizing them to do so. Although each state constitution outlined an independent process, most militia units were organized around a company of 50 men and under the command of one officer.[12] When the federal government (referred to during this period as the "General Government") needed to mobilize the militias, it would send each state a requested quota of militia companies or regiments. That quota would filter its way down to the militia companies, where the officer in charge would direct a gathering of all the men in the company. The quotas were usually for a small portion of the company's overall

---

[12] *Official Report of the Proceedings and Debates of the Third Constitutional Convention of Ohio Assembled in the City of Columbus on Tuesday May 13, 1873*, Cleveland, Ohio: W.S. Robison & Company, 1874, p. 355; *The Second Constitution of the State of New York*, Article II, Section 2, 1821.

strength, and the commanding officer would often first ask for volunteers. If he was unable to furnish the requested number of men, he had the authority under state laws (and the 1792 Militia Act, which compelled all men between 18 and 45 to militia service) to draft additional militia members into active service. Once a sufficient number of men were designated, they would then join a new "Common Militia" company organized as a composite of multiple town militias that were selected in the same way.[13] Common Militia units that were raised for federal service were limited to use only within the United States and for a maximum of three months, as stipulated in the 1792 Militia Act.

In addition to the federalized Common Militia, states could raise purely volunteer units, which could be used for service longer than three months and outside the United States. These volunteer units were raised by the states in similar ways to the compulsory militia described above. However, because they were raised based on calls by the federal government, which provided the volunteers with contractual terms for a length of service exceeding three months and potentially on foreign soil, they were not organized under the standing federal and state militia laws; rather, they were formed by the state militia systems under the leadership of state governors and, upon entering into federal service, fell under the armies clause of the Constitution. It was these types of volunteer units that provided the bulk of the manpower to fight the Mexican War, Civil War, and the Spanish-American War.

As the 19th century progressed and the Native American threat abated—a change that meant most Americans saw little need for compulsory militia service—a different type of militia referred to as the *Volunteer Militias* began to replace the Common Militias. The term reflected participants' voluntary commitment to training and organization; unlike the Common Militia described above, Volunteer Militia units were not organized by the states under the 1792 Militia Act but were instead formed by civilian men interested in military affairs and traditions who were seeking the camaraderie of other like-minded men. Despite their independent origins, the states did rely on the Volunteer Militias for law enforcement and to fulfill federal requests for militia units, and most units looked to their states for official recognition. However, the overall numbers of these Volunteer Militia units were small relative to the number of organized volunteers that would emerge in the 1880s.[14]

The War of 1812 revealed the structural weakness of the federal government's reliance on the state militia units. The system was slow and inefficient; although more than 400,000 regulars and militiamen (the vast majority being militia) fought for at least a portion of the war, the Army never totaled more than 70,000 men at one time, with 35,000 regulars and an equal number of militias and volunteers. The failure in 1792

---

[13] William D. Pratt, *A History of the National Guard of Indiana: From the Beginning of the Militia System in 1787 to the Present Time, Including the Services of Indiana Troops in the War with Spain*, Indianapolis, Ind.: W. D. Pratt, Printer and Binder, 1901.

[14] For a good description of the militia systems in practice, see Mahon, 1985.

and 1795 to establish either a single training requirement or a mechanism to enforce state training and equipment standards ensured that the few men who did fight often lacked sufficient preparation or arms. The U.S. Army's relative weakness against a professional army was made humiliatingly clear in August 1814, when it was shown to be powerless to stop a well-trained British regular force of approximately 5,000 men from burning a number of buildings in the nation's capital, including the White House.[15] Table 3.1 shows the different types of American militia in the 19th century and how they were organized and used, as well as their legal basis and historical context.[16]

The trauma of British Regulars burning Washington, combined with the difficulties in raising adequate militia and the Regular Army's recruitment problems, galvanized Federalist policymakers to advocate for new ways to increase the size and fighting effectiveness of the Army. Secretary of War James Monroe recommended a national draft premised on the Constitution's "raise and support armies" clause. Although the 1814 proposal failed by a single vote, his recommendation was an important first step in establishing a principle of universal civic responsibility that held virtually all American men to serve when called into not only the state militia but also the Federal Army as part of what would come to be called the "national forces." George Washington first used the term *national forces* in his 1783 *Sentiments on a Peace Establishment* to differentiate between a man's civic duty to serve in the state militias and his principled duty to serve in a national army. Thus, Secretary of War Monroe in 1814 premised his call for a national draft on the "raise and support armies" clause. Five decades later and two years into the American Civil War, the Union Congress (soon after the Confederate Congress) proclaimed it the duty of American men to serve in the "National Forces." This distinction is important because it illustrates Congress's gradual movement away from a reliance on the militia clause and to the "raise and support armies" clause to expand the army, and the use of the term *national forces* to manifest it.[17]

---

[15] Pisney, 1950; Weigley, 1967, p. 121.

[16] This table is based on a strictly historical rationale, especially when it concerns the links between these 19th century militia units and the present. However, we also acknowledge that the U.S. Army has created linkages from present-day Army units back to previous militia units and that this chart states there is no linkage. For example, the U.S. Army's Center of Military History provides a direct lineage to the first Militia Regiment established by law in the colony of Massachusetts in 1636 to an actively serving Army National Guard unit of today. Using the masterful 1982 essay by eminent military historian Sir Michael Howard on the uses and abuses of history ("The Use and Abuse of History," *The Royal United Services Institute (RUSI) Journal*, Vol. 138, No. 1, 1993), we posit that both approaches have value. Ours provides linkages and breaks from the past as a way to inform the study of history. The other approach, which links current National Guard units to compulsory and volunteer militias of previous eras, also has important value. As Sir Michael argues, that kind of history is important for establishing proud traditions and heritages from links to earlier eras that help to establish esprit de corps in present-day Army outfits. We argue that one is not superior to the other; they each simply have different purposes.

[17] Washington, (1783) 2011; *The Debates and Proceedings in the Congress of the United States, Thirteenth Congress, Third Session*, Washington, D.C.: Government Printing Office, 1814, pp. 483–496 Jack Franklin Leach, *Conscription in the United States: Historical Background*, Rutland, Vt.: C. E. Tuttle Pub. Co., 1952, p. 35; Leonard W. Levy, *Jefferson & Civil Liberties: The Darker Side*, revised ed., New York: Quadrangle, 1973.

Table 3.1
19th Century Militias and Volunteer Forces

Type of Force	Organization	Legal Basis	Use	Historical Period of Existence	Links to Present Day
Militia manpower pool (mostly white men)	Was not organized and is referred to in current law as the "unorganized militia." It was composed of all free able-bodied males between 18 and 45 years of age.	1792 Militia Act and state laws stipulating all adult free men's liability for militia service.	Was the manpower base for the various militias described below, both voluntary and compulsory.	Originated in the first American settlements in Virginia and Massachusetts and runs to the present day.	Title 32 (The National Guard) and Title 10, Subtitle A (The Army) both stipulate that American men ages 18–45 are in the "unorganized militia."
Compulsory militia (also referred to as the common militia)	Individual states required all men to be on militia musters and to meet for training as part of a militia company of approximately 60 men several times per year. Militia companies were often formed into regiments. By state and federal law, the common militia's service was limited to 3 months.	1792 Militia Act and state laws stipulating all adult free men's liability for militia service.	States used the compulsory militias for local law enforcement, defense, and Indian fighting. In times of war or insurrection, the federal government would assign quotas to states for militia units. Local militia captains would muster their men and organize a small number of volunteers or conscripts. The newly formed militia unit would be under federal service for up to 3 months.	Began in the first American settlements of Virginia and Massachusetts but had severely atrophied to the point that fewer and fewer states required men to muster regularly for training; by the 1840s, compulsory militia muster drill was a rarity.	None.

Table 3.1—Continued

Type of Force	Organization	Legal Basis	Use	Historical Period of Existence	Links to Present Day
State-sanctioned volunteer militia	Men interested in military affairs and the camaraderie of other like-minded men formed volunteer militia units independent of the state-generated common militias. They could be used in federal service for longer than 3 months.	State and local laws authorized governors, mayors, magistrates, etc., to utilize volunteer militia units. Their service on foreign soil during the Mexican-American War was founded on the Constitution's "raise and support armies" clause because they were brought into federal service as volunteers.	These volunteer militias were often called on by state governors for a variety of uses, including law enforcement and the escorting of dignitaries. Equally important, state governors offered these volunteer militias to meet federal quotas for the Mexican-American War and the Civil War.	The first volunteer militia was established in Boston in 1638. More developed in the 18th century. Volunteer militias were used extensively in the Mexican-American War and were the first militia units to respond to President Lincoln's call in the spring of 1861. Starting in the late 1870s, new volunteer militias began to form and call themselves "Guards" or "National Guards," increasingly under state control.	The modern National Guard traces its historical roots to the volunteer militias that emerged in the 1870s after the Civil War.
Volunteer militia and volunteer forces for federal service generated by state militia systems	The federal government issued calls to states to organize a quota of volunteers into regiments for federal service. These volunteer militias could serve for longer than 3 months in times of war.	1792 Militia Act, state militia laws, and the Constitution's "raise and support armies" clause.	Volunteer militias were used inconsistently during the War of 1812, but constitutional barriers limited their use beyond U.S. borders limited their utility. During the Mexican-American War, volunteer militias were locally organized, but the states could use them to meet federal quotas in times of war for 1–3 years.	The apex for volunteer militias and volunteer forces was during the Civil War, when the early armies of the war from the North and South consisted overwhelmingly of volunteer units.	None.

Table 3.1—Continued

Type of Force	Organization	Legal Basis	Use	Historical Period of Existence	Links to Present Day
Civil War Union volunteer regiments (the sheer number of volunteers relative to other U.S. wars makes this a separate category)	Through Lincoln's executive order, the federal government issued quotas to states for "volunteers." States then relied on local systems to organize regiments of infantry, cavalry, artillery, etc. These volunteer units were technically "militia" because, under the 1792 Militia Act, all men ages 18–45 were part of the "unorganized militia."	The 1792 Militia Act was amended twice during the Civil War. The authority to call on the militia was based on Article 1, Section 8's provisions to suppress insurrection. With the March 1863 Enrollment Act, volunteers (and draftees) were brought into federal service under the "raise and support armies" clause.	After organizing volunteer regiments and, in some cases, providing initial training, states sent them to rendezvous points where the regiments were brought into federal service and assigned to higher brigades for service in the various theaters of war. Terms of service ranged from 6 months to 3 years to the full duration of the war.	The Civil War. Although the states produced these kinds of volunteer units for the Mexican-American War and, in a more limited sense, the War of 1812, the aggregate size of the Union Army, made up largely of volunteer regiments, makes the Civil War distinct from previous U.S. wars.	None.
Federal volunteers, "with special qualifications," for the Spanish-American War	The 1898 act for Army expansion authorized the federal government to organize, directly, volunteers with "special qualifications." As a result, three federal cavalry regiments were raised (one of which was Leonard Wood's and Teddy Roosevelt's 1st Volunteer Cavalry). These regiments were formed in territories rather than states in part because there would have been limited senior field and commanding officer positions if the regiments had been formed by the states using their existing National Guard units.	The 1898 act passed to expand the Army stipulated that these federal volunteer cavalry regiments would be organized in the territories directly by the federal government under the Constitution's armies clause. They were intentionally formed in the territories to bypass problems with the individual states and their governors, who were forming militia units for volunteering into federal service.	Only one volunteer cavalry regiment was actually formed: Wood and Roosevelt's 1st Volunteer Cavalry, which deployed with Regular Army forces to Cuba, was brigaded with a Regular Army cavalry division, and fought at the Battle of San Juan Hill.	The Spanish-American War from April to August 1898. They were formed using existing militia companies and individual volunteers in the territories of Arizona, New Mexico, and Oklahoma and consolidated their training in San Antonio, Texas. However, men from the northeast who were friends of Roosevelt also volunteered as enlisted men and officers.	None.

The harsh memories of the sacking of the nation's capital caused Monroe's successor, Secretary of War John C. Calhoun, to put forward to Congress a new plan in 1820 to address many shortcomings revealed by the war. Calhoun called for the state militias to be removed entirely from Army mobilization schemes, and relegated both the Volunteer and Common Militias to state functions only. In place of the militias, Calhoun proposed an "expansible army" plan that aimed to balance the need to maintain a professional Regular Army with the cultural and political pressure to keep it relatively small in peacetime. Calhoun envisioned a structure in which regiments would be manned in peacetime by a full complement of commissioned and noncommissioned officers but reduced enlisted strength. When the need arose, the federal government could increase the size of the Army by recruiting and enlisting volunteers directly into the Regular Army and would not need to rely on the states to produce militia units. These federal volunteers recruited into the Regular Army could then be assigned into existing half-strength Regular Army regiments to bring them to full strength, each led by trained by Regular officers and noncommissioned officers. Most of Calhoun's expansible army plan was rejected by Congress because it would have put in place an increased number of Regular Army officers for increasing the size of regiments and for a newly organized army staff, which would have increased the plan's necessary funding. Calhoun's plan was also politically sensitive issue because it came about at a time when fierce individualism and an expanding American commercial market honed the idea of the self-made man who had little time for militia duties. Congress was especially attuned to this attitude, even as numerous Presidents and Secretaries of War, like Calhoun, called for Army reform. With Congress unwilling to act on Calhoun's expansible army plan, the ability of the Army to increase in size for future wars was left to the established system of state-provided militia units.[18]

The state militia system's ability to help the federal government increase the size of the Army was tested again in 1846 with the start of the Mexican-American War. To fight an offensive war on foreign soil, Congress expanded the overall size of the Army, which at the time stood at 8,000 soldiers, by filling out the ranks of the Regulars through direct enlistment and by calling on the states to provide militia units. Unlike in 1812, the states' first recourse to meet federal quotas was to use their Volunteer Militia units. However, the preponderance of forces produced from the states came from new state volunteer units raised for federal service. These Volunteer Militias and new volunteer units were appealing to the federal government because they could serve on offensive campaigns on foreign soil. Moreover, because they were not organized under

---

[18] War Department, *Reduction of the Army*, Washington, D.C.: 16th Congress, Second Session, 1820; C. Vann Woodward, "The Age of Reinterpretation," *American Historical Review*, Vol. 66, No. 1, October 1960; Roger Spiller, "Calhoun's Expansible Army: The History of a Military Idea," *South Atlantic Quarterly*, Spring 1980; Samuel J. Watson, *Jackson's Sword: The Army Officer Corps on the American Frontier, 1810–1821*, Lawrence, Kan.: University Press of Kansas, 2012; William B. Skelton, *The United States Army, 1821–1837: An Institutional History*, PhD dissertation, Evanston, Ill.: Northwestern University, 1968.

the 1792 Militia Act, they could also be used in federal service for longer than three months.[19]

When the Civil War began in April 1861, a mere 13 years after the war with Mexico had ended, President Abraham Lincoln called on the states to provide 75,000 militiamen to suppress the rebellion. Northern states responded to this first call by sending existing and newly created Volunteer Militia units. As the war developed, the Union government struggled to keep the Army at full strength. Desperate to provide manpower, it relied on a complex mosaic of methods to maintain the Union Army as a fighting force:

1. A slightly increased Regular Army.
2. State Volunteer Militia units that existed at the start of the war organized on their own volition and volunteered for federal service.
3. Individual volunteers drawn from both those who were actively "enrolled" in the few remaining prewar compulsory militia units and those who were a part of the militia manpower pool; these newly created state volunteer units made up the bulk of the Union Army. (Volunteers also made up the mainstay of the Confederate Army.)
4. Civilian men who continued to serve in state militia units at home for local defense (such as the Pennsylvania state militia called out for Lee's invasion of Pennsylvania in July 1863).
5. A limited number of men drafted under the March 1863 Enrollment Act (discussed below).

Yet the states using these methods increasingly struggled to satisfy the federal quotas placed on them, and in July 1862 Congress passed an act authorizing the President to direct state governors to draft men into new regiments for federal service. This directive in effect drew on the compulsory elements of universal military obligation

[19] Mahon, 1983; Marcus Cunliffe, *Soldiers & Civilians: The Martial Spirit in America, 1775–1865*, Boston: Little, Brown, 1968; William H. Riker, *Soldiers of the States: The Role of the National Guard in American Democracy*, Washington, D.C.: Public Affairs Press, 1957; Stephen A. Carney, *Guns Along the Rio Grande Palo Alto and Resaca de la Palma*, Washington, D.C.: U.S. Army Center of Military History, 2005; Henry Lee, *The Militia of the United States: What It Has Been, What It Should Be*, Boston: Marvin & Son, 1864; Robert Johannsson, *To the Halls of the Montezuma: The Mexican War in the American Imagination*, New York: Oxford University Press, 1974; K. Jack Bauer and H. Sutton James, Jr., *The Mexican War, 1846–1848*, New York: Macmillan, 1974, pp. 57–58; Kreidberg and Henry, 1955, pp. 74–75; Samuel J. Watson, *Peacekeepers and Conquerors: The Army Officer Corps on the American Frontier, 1821–1846*, Lawrence, Kan.: Kansas University Press, 2013; William B. Skelton, *An American Profession of Arms: The Army Officer Corps, 1784–1861*, Lawrence, Kan.: University Press of Kansas, 1992; K. Jack Bauer, "The Battles on the Rio Grande: Palo Alto and Resaca de la Palma, 8–9 May 1846," in William Stoft and Charles Heller, eds., *1776–1965, America's First Battles*, Lawrence, Kan.: Kansas University Press, 1984; Ulysses S. Grant, *Personal Memoirs*, New York: The Modern Library, 1885.

in the already existing 1792 Militia Act. The governors never put the August law into effect, partly because they managed, in the end, to meet their federal quotas.[20]

Nonetheless, manpower shortages continued, and in March 1863 Congress, frustrated by its reliance on the states to provide Volunteer regiments, passed what is commonly referred to as the Enrollment Act. This act furthered the shift already under way whereby Congress began to rely more and more on the "raise and support armies" clause of the Constitution to increase the size of the Army rather than the militia clause. The Enrollment Act authorized the federal government to bypass state governors and the state militia systems to draft men directly into the Union Army. It did so by stipulating, under the "raise and support armies" clause, that all adult males were liable for service in the federal "national forces."[21] The act laid the groundwork for subsequent laws passed in the 20th century to enable the federal government to generate the mass armies required for industrial warfare.

Even though conscription played a role in manning the Union Army in the North, when the war ended, Union veterans reentered civilian life with a firm belief that it was the Union men who had volunteered in the hundreds of thousands who won the war, a view epitomized in former Union Army General John Logan's 1887 *The Volunteer Soldier of America*. Yet just as the Civil War popularized faith in the volunteer tradition, it also destroyed the antebellum militia in America. In its place, veterans from both the North and South began to form in the 1870s new Volunteer Militia units

---

[20] The two relevant acts are U.S. Statutes at Large, An Act to Provide for the Suppression of Rebellion Against and Resistance to the Laws of the United States, and to Amend the Act Entitled "An Act to Provide for Calling Forth the Militia to Execute the Laws of the Union" Passed February Twenty-Eight, Seventeen Hundred and Ninety-Five, 37th Congress, 1st Session, Chapter 25, July 29, 1861 (12 Stat. 281); and U.S. Statutes at Large, An Act to Amend the Act Calling Forth the Militia to Execute the Laws of the Union, Suppress Insurrections, and Repel Invasions, Approved February Twenty-Eight, Seventeen Hundred and Ninety-five, and the Acts Amendatory Thereof, and for Other Purposes, Thirty-Seventh Congress, Session II, Chapter 201, July 17, 1862 (12 Stat. 597). William Best Hesseltine, *Lincoln and the War Governors*, New York: A.A. Knopf, 1948; Fred A. Shannon, *The Organization and Administration of the Union Army*, Bethesda, Md.: University Publications of America, 1994; William L. Shaw, *The Civil War Federal Conscription and Exemption System*, Washington, D.C.: Judge Advocates Association, 1962a. For Confederate militia, see Albert Burton Moore, *Conscription and Conflict in the Confederacy*, New York: The Macmillan Company, 1924, pp. 1–11; William C. Harris, *Leroy Pope Walker: Confederate Secretary of War*, Tuscaloosa, Ala.: Confederate Pub. Co., 1962, pp. 56–71; William L. Shaw, "The Confederate Conscription and Exemption Acts," *American Journal of Legal History*, Vol. 6, No. 4, October, 1962b, pp. 368–405; E. Merton Coulter and Frank L. Owsley, "The Confederate States of America, 1861–1865," *The Journal of Economic History*, Vol. 10, No. 2, 1950. For the Confederate Army, see Joseph T. Glatthaar, *General Lee's Army: From Victory to Collapse*, New York: Free Press, 2008.

[21] U.S. Statutes at Large, An Act for Enrolling and Calling Out the National Forces, and for Other Purposes, Thirty-Seventh Congress, Session III, Chapter 75, March 3, 1863 (12 Stat. 781); James W. Geary, *We Need Men: The Union Draft in the Civil War*, DeKalb, Ill.: Northern Illinois University Press, 1991; Shaw, 1962a; Eugene C. Murdock, *Patriotism Limited, 1862–1865: The Civil War Draft and the Bounty System*, Kent, Ohio: The Kent State University Press, 1967; Iver Bernstein, *The New York City Draft Riots: Their Significance for American Society and Politics in the Age of the Civil War*, Oxford, UK: Oxford University Press, 1990; Allan Nevins, *The War for the Union: War Becomes Revolution, 1862–1863, Volume I*, New York: Scribner, 1959.

commonly referred to as either Guards or National Guards.[22] Governors also saw the utility of these new volunteer National Guard units, as the need for a state military force to deal with growing labor unrest and other state and local matters grew. It was in this volunteer militia tradition, as National Guard officer Frederick P. Todd noted in a prize-winning 1941 essay in a widely read military journal, "that the origin of the present National Guard" can be found.[23]

Yet there was disagreement about the purpose and allegiance of the National Guard units. By the mid-1880s, three views emerged. Some Guardsman argued that Guard units should remain exclusively under state control and be entirely independent of the federal government and Regular Army. They highlighted the need in many states for a military force to manage labor unrest and other law enforcement tasks. Proponents of sole state control also pointed out the risks of militarism and federal intervention in state affairs. In a sense, this position was the lonely survivor of the antebellum states' rights school, which by the late 1880s was fading.[24]

Their state-centric viewpoint was countered by a second group of Guardsmen who wanted to sever all ties to the states and become a federal reserve force to the Army. This group embraced the professionalist mindset and welcomed the opportunity to be federally "well regulated," to the extent that it meant they would be recognized as playing an important role and federally funded accordingly. These Guardsmen also argued that multiple states would never be able to organize disparate state military forces that could fight alongside the Regular Army as a first-line reserve without strong centralized control by the federal government.[25]

A third group of Guardsmen split the difference between the state-centric and pro-federal camps. This group of Guardsmen wanted the Guard units of the several states to be recognized as an integral part of the nation's "first-line defenses" alongside the Regular Army, as opposed to being a local security force that might occasionally be called upon for national service. However, this group of Guardsmen also wanted to remain linked to the states but simultaneously enjoy higher levels of federal funding,

---

[22] Cooper, 1993, pp. 86–89. For a contemporaneous argument for the volunteer tradition, see John Alexander Logan and Cornelius Ambrose Logan, *The Volunteer Soldier of America*, Chicago and New York: R.S. Peale & Co., 1887.

[23] Herbert Barry, "In What Way Can the National Guard Be Modified So as to Make It an Effective Reserve to the Regular Army in Both War and Peace?" *Journal of Military Service Institution of the United States*, Vol. 39, July–December 1906, p. 197; Mahon, 1983, p. 108.

[24] Frederick P. Todd, "Our National Guard: An Introduction to Its History," published in two parts in *Military Affairs*, Vol. 5, No. 2, Summer 1941a, and Vol. 5, No. 3, Autumn 1941b.

[25] Todd, 1941a, 1941b; Derthick, 1965; Doubler, 2001; Jack D. Foner, *The United States Soldier Between Two Wars: Army Life and Reforms, 1865–1898*, New York: Humanities Press, 1970; Jerry M. Cooper, *The Army and Civil Disorder: Federal Military Intervention in Labor Disputes, 1877–1900*, PhD dissertation, Madison: University of Wisconsin, 1971; Brian Dexter Fowles, *A Guard in Peace and War: The History of the Kansas National Guard, 1854–1987*, Manhattan, Kan.: Sunflower University, 1989; Cooper, 1998.

because they saw themselves in the nation's first-line defenses as a reserve force to the Army.[26] It was members of this third camp who first conceived the modern National Guard as a dual state and federal reserve force. Here was the intellectual core of a desire to form a reserve component to the Army by combining the "militia" and "raise and support armies" clauses of the Constitution. The National Guard Association was formed in 1878 to champion this particular vision for the modern National Guard. It would come to statutory fruition in 1933, as we explain below.[27]

In the decades after the American Civil War, Guardsmen were not the only advocates of reform. A number of Regular Army officers were also calling for reform of the Regular Army, the system that increased the size of the Army in wartime, and the laws that governed the process. One of the most important of these officers was Colonel Emory Upton, a brilliant Civil War veteran who was known for his courage under fire and innovative tactics. After the war, he toured Europe and Asia and studied the continents' armies. Upon his return, Upton published *The Armies of Asia and Europe* (1878), which contained a concluding section that called for a federally run system of mobilization that no longer relied on the states to produce poorly trained and disparately equipped men for battle. It was in the European countries of Germany and England where Upton was exposed to the popularly used term *military policy*. Indeed, Upton returned from Europe with the firm idea that the United States needed a real, extant military policy and that he would be the one to provide it.

To demonstrate what he saw as the futility of the state-centric system for mobilizing reserve forces to increase the size of the Army, Upton turned to the study of American military history. Between 1879 and his untimely death in 1881, Upton produced a manuscript titled *The Military Policy of the United States*, in which he methodically laid out in painstaking detail using primary evidence what he saw as the folly of relying on state militia systems to increase the size of the Army rather than a mechanism under sole federal control. Although his early death from suicide meant that the manuscript was not published until 1904, by Secretary of War Elihu Root (as discussed below),

---

[26] Volunteers of America, *Proceedings of the Convention of National Guards*, St. Louis, Mo., October 1, 1879; Derthick, 1965; Doubler, 2001; Riker, 1957; Jim Dan Hill, *The Minute Man in Peace and War: A History of the National Guard*, Harrisburg, Pa.: Stackpole Books, 1964.

[27] For a succinct statement that draws a direct line between the modern Guard and the Constitution's militia and even Washington's 1783 Peace Establishment plan, see National Guard Association of the United States (NGAUS) President Major General Ellard Walsh, "Address to the Army War College (February 1953)," in Ellard A. Walsh and Edgar C. Erickson, *The Nation's National Guard*, Washington, D.C.: National Guard Association of the United States, 1954. For counter views by Constitutional scholars who argue that the modern National Guard of today is not the militias envisioned by the Constitution, see H. Richard Uviller and William G. Merkel, *The Militia and the Right to Arms, or, How the Second Amendment Fell Silent*, Durham, N.C.: Duke University Press, 2002, p. 144; Bahar, 2014, pp. 557–559; Engdahl, 1971, p. 63; Randy E. Barnett, "Was the Right to Keep and Bear Arms Conditioned on Service in an Organized Militia?" *Texas Law Review*, Vol. 83, 2004, p. 274; Stephen I. Vladeck, "The Calling Forth Clause and the Domestic Commander in Chief," *Cardozo Law Review*, Vol. 29, No. 3, 2008: Jason Mazzone, "The Commander in Chief," *Notre Dame Law Review*, Vol. 83, 2007–2008.

the work's title and Upton's ideas resonated with many Regular Army officers and a number of political leaders interested in Army reform. Indeed, the title, *The Military Policy of the United States*, became the stock term of art for the next 70 years in discussing Army reform.

It was in those future discussions and debates where certain Army reformers after the Spanish-American War and in the first half of the 20th century would characterize Upton's ideas as alien to American political and social culture and out of date with the strategic challenges presented by World Wars I and II. Yet Upton carried out his research and made his arguments for Army reform to solve the problems of Army expansion that he saw from the perspective of the late 1870s. Congress, though, not only initially rejected Upton's reforms but also chose not to enact any kind of legislation that would bring about Army reform or establish at least the beginnings of a *military policy* for the Army. Less than 20 years after Upton's death in 1881, the Spanish-American War would manifest in spades the problem of not having such a policy.

CHAPTER FOUR

From the Spanish-American War to Total War

Congress declared war on Spain on April 25, 1898. Shortly thereafter, on April 22, 1898, Congress passed an "Act to Provide for Temporarily Increasing the Peace Establishment of the United States in Time of War," authorizing a mobilization of volunteers and National Guard units of the several states to increase the size of the Army for war. Critically, the 1898 act evoked the exact language used in the 1863 Enrollment Act's reference to the "National Forces" of the United States. According to both the 1863 and 1898 acts, the "National Forces" consisted of "all able bodied male citizens of the United States . . . between the ages of eighteen and forty-five years of age." Recall that the Militia Act of 1792 had established in law the universal military obligation of virtually all able-bodied males between 18 and 45 to be members of the militia and susceptible to duty in the militia to repel invasions or deal with other domestic matters. Now, Congress established in law a universal military obligation for the country's males between 18 and 45 to perform military duty "in the service of the *United States*." Whereas the Militia Act only allowed for domestic militia duty and was premised on the militia clause of the Constitution, the 1898 act established an obligation for potential service in foreign wars under the "raise and support armies" clause of the Constitution. Although the federal government would ultimately not use the option to fight Spain, the 1898 act provided that conscription could be used if necessary.[1] The 1898 act represents another point on the path Congress had been taking to expand the Army for war based on the armies clause rather than the militia clause.

The Spanish-American War proved to be a major turning point that inaugurated the second important period for the evolution of U.S. military policy. The United States' capture of Cuba, Puerto Rico, and the Philippines meant that the nation now

---

[1] U.S. Statutes at Large, An Act to Provide for Temporarily Increasing the Military Establishment of the United States in Time of War, and for Other Purposes, Fifty-Fifth Congres, Session II, Chapter 187, April 22, 1898 (30 Stat. 361); 12 Stat. 781; Graham A. Cosmas, *An Army for Empire: The United States Army in the Spanish-American War*, Columbia, Mo.: University of Missouri Press, 1971; Gerald F. Linderman, *The Mirror of War: American Society and the Spanish-American War*, Ann Arbor, Mich.: University of Michigan Press, 1974; Jerry Cooper, "National Guard Reform, The Army, and the Spanish-American War: The View from Wisconsin," *Military Affairs*, Vol. 42, No. 1, January 1978; Kenneth Roy Bailey, *A Search for Identity: The West Virginia National Guard, 1877–1921*, dissertation, Ohio State University, 1976; Kreidberg and Henry, 1955.

had significant overseas responsibilities. Another result was the public debacle of mobilizing and transporting an unprepared Regular Army and National Guard to first fight Spain in Cuba and subsequently occupy and pacify the Philippines—an embarrassment that led Secretary of War Elihu Root and others to conclude that significant reforms were necessary. Working with the War Department, the National Guard, and Congress, and heavily influenced by Upton's *The Military Policy of the United States*, Root moved to modernize the Army and the laws that governed it.[2]

Much of the impetus for reform reflected professionalists' preference for a robust Regular Army and federally trained and resourced state militias. Indeed, it was during this period that part of the National Guard came to fully embrace the professionalist mindset and argue that it needed better training, equipment, and organization to function as a first-line defense reserve force.[3] Yet even though it embraced its role as a reserve force to the Army, and even though Congress had been increasing its reliance on the armies clause to expand the size of the Army in war, the Guard clung to its perceived identity as the heir to the compulsory militia tradition evoked by the militia clause. In effect, the Guard sought to elevate its relationship with the federal government while insisting that it remained a dual force subordinate to both the states and the federal government.[4]

The keystone of the post–Spanish-American War reforms was a piece of 1903 legislation titled "An Act to Promote the Efficiency of the Militia, and for Other Purposes," often referred to as the Military Act of 1903 or the Dick Act after one its proponents, Congressman Charles Dick of Ohio. Charles Dick was not only a congressman, he was also was a long-serving Guardsman from Ohio who had served in the Spanish-American War. He had risen through the ranks, and, at the signing of the act that bears his name in 1903, he was a major general in the Ohio National Guard

---

[2] On other measures of Army reform, see U.S. Statutes, An Act to Increase the Efficiency of the Permanent Military Establishment of the United States, Fifty-Sixth Congress, Session II, Chapter 192, February 2, 1901 (31 Stat. 748); Secretary of War and the Bureau Chiefs, *Annual Report of the War Department, 1902*, Vol. 2, Washington, D.C.: U.S. House of Representatives, 1903; William Harding Carter and James Wolcott Wadsworth, Jr., "Creation of the American General Staff, Personal narrative of the General Staff System of the American Army, by Major General William Harding Carter, Presented by Mr. Wadsworth, January 22, 1924—Referred to the Committee on Printing," 1924. On Root and the Root reforms, see Elihu Root, "Elihu Root to Lieutenant General S. B. M. Young, September 17, 1916," in Robert Bacon and James Brown Scott, eds., *The Military and Colonial Policy of the United States: Addresses and Reports*, New York: AMS Press, 1970; Jerry Cooper, *The Rise of the National Guard: The Evolution of the American Militia, 1865–1920*, Lincoln: University of Nebraska Press, 1997; Louis Cantor, *The Creation of the Modern National Guard: The Dick Militia Act of 1903*, PhD dissertation, Durham, N.C.: Duke University, 1963; Elbridge Colby, "The Status of the National Guard," *Central Law Journal*, January 1925; Phillip Jessup, *Elihu Root*, two volumes, New York: Dodd Mead, 1938.

[3] For a clear enunciation of this view, see "Militia and Army: The Secretary of War Favors Closer Relations," *Washington Post*, December 1, 1902.

[4] Interstate National Guard Association, *Fourth Annual Convention*, Washington, D.C., January 20–22, 1902, Washington, D.C.: National Guard Museum.

and president of the National Guard Association.[5] The 1903 law, which replaced the 1792 Militia Act, recognized the National Guard of the many states as the federally recognized "organized militia" of the several states, something the 1792 act never did. The 1903 act directed the states' National Guards to develop within five years the same "organization, armament, and discipline" as the Regular Army, with some exceptions. Importantly, the act stipulated that the Guard's purpose was to defend against foreign invasions and suppress rebellions against the laws of the United States. Thus, the law organized the National Guard as state militia under federal statute and premised on the militia clause of the Constitution. The Dick Act certainly envisioned this newly organized and federally recognized state militia as a reserve force for Army expansion. The Act said nothing about sending the National Guard as the organized militia abroad to fight foreign wars. However, because the Dick Act organized the Guard under the militia clause, the question of whether the Guard could be used outside the borders of the United States to fight foreign wars produced a contentious legal debate over the next 15 years.[6]

Another important step occurred in April 1908, when Congress passed an act to establish a "medical reserve corps" for the Army. This act sought to improve medical care after the debacle of the Army's deployment to Cuba in 1898, where disease and antiquated medical care contributed to the high death toll. The April 1908 act was premised on the "raise and support armies" clause of the Constitution.[7] The act established the legal origins of today's U.S. Army Reserve. Moreover, in establishing a federal reserve independent of the states' organized militias—the National Guards—it reflected an effort to resolve an intrinsic difficulty for the Army: how to maintain limits on the size of the Regular Army while simultaneously maintaining an adequately large pool of trained soldiers and units solely under federal control premised on the "raise and support armies" clause of the Constitution. The National Guards could provide these units, but strong concerns about the legality of deploying Guard units to fight on foreign soil persisted. Another concern was that the Guard, when not federalized, was under the control of the states and their governors, which meant in practice that the principle of unity of command under one centralized authority—the President—so important to Regular Army officers, would be compromised by the dual control role of the governors.[8]

---

[5] U.S. Statutes at Large, An Act to Promote the Efficiency of the Militia, and for Other Purposes, Fifty-Seventh Congress, Session II, Chapter 196, January 21, 1903 (32 Stat. 775).

[6] In 1912, for example, U.S. Attorney General George W. Wickersham argued that the National Guard as organized under the militia clause via the Dick Act could not be deployed to fight foreign wars; it would be, according to Wickersham, "unconstitutional." See *Office of Attorney General*, Vol. 29, 1912; Hirsch, 1988, pp. 944–946.

[7] U.S. Statutes at Large, An Act to Increase the Efficiency of the Medical Department of the United States Army, Sixtieth Congress, Session I, Chapter 150, April 23, 1908 (35 Stat. 66).

[8] For examples of the varying viewpoints on this topic, see Frederic Louis Huidekoper and William H. Taft, *Is the United States Prepared for War?* New York: North American Review Pub. Co., 1907, pp. 391–407; William H.

With the establishment of a federal Medical Reserve Corps, a growing disagreement emerged between the War Department and the National Guard of the several states (as well as their respective allies in Congress) over just what the proper military policy should be with regard to a reserve component (or components) for the Army. In May 1908, only a month after it established the Medical Reserve Corps, Congress passed an amendment to the Dick Act stipulating that, if the Army needed to become larger in times of war and national emergencies, the National Guards would be called forth into federal service in "advance" of any federal volunteer units raised by the federal government.[9] This was a signal to the War Department to rely on the National Guard before federal volunteers were sought to expand the Army by increasing its size. The act also stoked the debate over the constitutionality of deploying the National Guard of the several states that were federally organized under the militia clause overseas to fight foreign wars by stipulating that the states' Guards, when called to federal service, could be used "either within or without the territory of the United States."[10]

Thus, these two laws, passed within one month of each other in 1908, reflected the two sides of the debate over what the Army and, in particular, the Army reserve components should be. Should the reserve components be made up by the National Guard as the primary reserve for the Army with a dual constitutional status or as a purely federal force?[11] The debate got to the heart over the tension between which of the two constitutional clauses—the "raise and support armies" clause and the militia clause—should be the defining clause for the Army, or whether a combination of both

---

Carter, "When Diplomacy Fails," *The North American Review*, Vol. 187, No. 626, 1908, pp. 23–33. Also see Timothy K. Nenninger, *The Leavenworth Schools and the Old Army: Education, Professionalism, and the Officer Corps of the United States Army, 1881–1918*, Westport, Conn.: Greenwood Press, 1978; James S. Pettit, "How Far Does Democracy Affect the Organization of Our Armies, and How Can Its Influence Be Most Effectually Utilized?" *Journal of the Military Service Institute of the United States*, No. 38, January–February 1906. A good history of the Army Reserve is Richard B. Crossland and James T. Currie, *Twice the Citizen: A History of the United States Army Reserve, 1908–1983*, Washington, D.C.: Office of the Chief, Army Reserve, 1984, p. 151.

[9] These types of volunteers, brought into the Army under federal auspices, were different from the Federal Volunteer Cavalry Regiments of the Spanish-American War in that they would volunteer for the Army as individuals across all states of the Union and be used to build new volunteer infantry units among other types to increase the size of the Army. The three regiments of Federal Volunteer Cavalry in the Spanish-American War were formed only in the then-existing territories and only to serve as federal cavalry.

[10] U.S. Statutes at Large, An Act to Further Amend the Act Entitled "An Act to Promote the Efficiency of the Militia and for Other Purposes, Approved January Twenty-First Nineteen Hundred and Three," Sixtieth Congress, Session I, Chapter 204, May 27, 1908 (35 Stat 399).

[11] General Staff, U.S. Department of War, *Report on the Organization of the Land Forces of the United States*, Washington, D.C.: U.S. Government Printing Office, 1912; Henry L. Stimson, *What Is the Matter with Our Army?* Washington, D.C.: U.S. Government Printing Office, 1912; Jonathan M. House, "John McAuley Palmer and the Reserve Components," *Parameters*, Vol. 12, No. 3, 1982; Holley and Palmer, 1982; Mabel E. Deutrich, *Struggle for Supremacy: The Career of General Fred C. Ainsworth*, Washington, D.C.: Public Affairs Press, 1962; John Patrick Finnegan, *Against the Specter of a Dragon; the Campaign for American Military Preparedness, 1914–1917*, Westport, Conn.: Greenwood Press, 1974.

should be used. The War Department and its allies clearly argued for the armies clause as the sole defining clause, while the National Guard and its advocates argued for both the armies and militia clauses.

In 1915, as World War I raged in Europe, Secretary of War Lindley Garrison and the Army's General Staff proposed a new Army policy that attempted to answer this question. Garrison and the War Department aimed to establish the basic structure needed for the Army to fight modern industrial war. In what came to be known as the "Continental Army" plan, they gave the missions of coastal and home defense to National Guard units of the several states and ended their role as a primary reserve in the first-line defense to the Regular Army. Garrison's plan called for a relatively large Regular Army backed by a larger force of close to half a million trained volunteers who would spend approximately three months a year on active duty. This Army would be commanded, organized, and trained by the Regular Army. It would maintain its ranks by creating a system that brought in volunteers who would spend three years in the Regular Army and then enter into a Federal Reserve pool of individual replacements. If the half-million-man Continental Army required an increase in size in a time of war, the individual replacement pool would facilitate that process. Of course, this proposal's potential expense and the alignment of the National Guard to a state militia force proved extremely controversial. President Woodrow Wilson eventually disavowed the plan. However, the sharp reaction the plan provoked can be read as evidence of continued disagreements over military policy and how best to organize a reserve component for the Army.[12]

Congress's response to the Continental Army Plan was the 1916 National Defense Act (NDA), which, like other post–Spanish-American War legislation, aimed to improve the nation's ability to mobilize the kind of forces appropriate for industrial-era expeditionary warfare. The NDA stipulated that the National Guard units of the several states, when federalized, would be a component of the U.S. Army under the "raise and support armies" clause.[13] The 1903 Dick Act, in contrast, had premised its federal recognition of the National Guard as the organized militia on the militia clause. The 1916 NDA did not, however, satisfy critics who, predicting future American involvement in the war in Europe, called for both sweeping reform of the Army and universal military training. Former Secretary of War Elihu Root, who had pushed the Dick Act

---

[12] U.S. General Staff, *Statement of Proper Military Policy for the United States*, Washington, D.C.: U.S. Government Printing Office, 1916; C. Joseph Bernardo and Eugene Hayward Bacon, *American Military Policy, Its Development Since 1775*, Harrisburg, Pa.: Military Service Pub. Co., 1955; Leonard Wood, *The Military Obligation of Citizenship*, Princeton, N.J.: Princeton University Press, 1915.

[13] Public Law 64-85, An Act for Making Further and More Effectual Provision for the National Defense, and for Other Purposes, June 3, 1916; Derthick, 1965; George S. Pappas, *Prudens Futuri: The U.S. Army War College, 1901–1967*, Carlisle Barracks, Pa.: Alumni Association of the U.S. Army War College, 1967; James E. Hewes, *From Root to McNamara: Army Organization and Administration, 1900–1963*, Washington, D.C.: Center of Military History, U.S. Army, 1975.

through Congress in 1903, had a change of mind about the National Guard in 1916. In September, only three months after Congress passed the 1916 NDA, Root voiced intense criticism of the use of the National Guard when federalized as the primary reserve to the Army:

> The National Guard system is not adequate and cannot be made adequate to meet the needs of the national defense. . . . [I]t is impossible to have an effective body of soldiers who serve two masters [state governors and the President] and are raised and organized to accomplish two different purposes [militia clause and raise and support armies clause].[14]

When the United States finally declared war on Germany in April 1917, President Wilson and the War Department quickly realized that although the 1916 NDA provided a minimum basis for rapidly increasing the size of the Army, it was insufficient for expanding the Army to the size planners believed necessary for the war. As a result, Congress passed the first national Selective Service Act in 1917, authorizing a national draft and making virtually all men of the appropriate age liable for military service.[15] The 1917 act premised conscription on the "raise and support armies" clause of the Constitution.

Some challenged the Selective Service Act on the legal grounds that a man could not be drafted into the federal army, since the 1903 Dick Act had already committed him as part of the unorganized militia. Others charged that the Selective Service Act was an infringement on individual liberty, since the militia clause offered limits on congressional authority to raise armies.

Legal challenges to the act went all the way to the Supreme Court, where Chief Justice Edward Douglass White wrote a unanimous opinion that upheld the Selective Service Act as constitutional and found that the militia clause did not limit Congress's ability to raise and support armies. In a historical examination of the nation's past drafts, White found that the means by which conscription was enforced had been "directly federal, and the force to be raised as a result of the draft was therefore typically national, as distinct from the call into active service of the militia as such."[16] In other words, the "raise and support armies" clause was superior to the militia clause when it came to organizing the U.S. military and fighting wars.[17] In the long term, the Supreme Court profoundly affected the originally established limits on constitutional

---

[14] Root, 1970.

[15] Public Law 65-12, An Act to Authorize the President to Increase Temporarily the Military Establishment of the United States, May 18, 1917.

[16] *Arver v. United States*, 245 U. S. 366, 386 (December 1918). Also known as the Selective Draft Law Cases.

[17] U.S. Statutes at Large, An Act to Authorize the President to Increase Temporarily the Military Establishment of the United States, Sixty-Fifth Congress, Session 1, Chapter 15, May 18, 1917 (40 Stat. 76); *Arver v. United States*, 245 U. S. 366, 386 (December 1918); Stephen I. Vladek, *The Calling Forth Clause and the Domestic Com-*

power. The Court's judgment gave judicial credence to a shift that had been occurring since the early 19th century as Congress progressively increased its reliance on the "raise and support armies" clause and decreased its dependence on the militia clause. Thus, the precedent was set for future conflicts, anchored firmly by judicial opinion of constitutional authority.

Two years after World War I's end, Congress passed the 1920 NDA, which preserved many aspects of the 1916 NDA.[18] For example, the National Guard was defined as only a part of the U.S. Army when federalized and in service of the United States. To become federalized, as in the 1916 Act, individual Guardsmen had to be drafted into federal service and, in turn, discharged from the militia. When not federalized, the Guard was recognized in federal statutes as the states' organized militia and thus tied to the militia clause of the Constitution. In theory and in practice, this meant that the War Department could devise plans to create its own federal reserve force, as it tried to do with the Continental Army plan in 1915.

There were alternative versions to the 1920 NDA from the one that was actually passed. Chair of the Senate Military Affairs Committee James Wadsworth, with the help of Army Colonel John McAuley Palmer, a West Point graduate and influential expert on military policy, put forward a bill that would have made fundamental changes to the 1916 NDA. The Wadsworth Bill called for peacetime universal military training of adult American men and proposed organizing the Guard under the armies clause of the Constitution and severing completely its link to the militia clause. The Guard would remain spread throughout all the states and territories so that it could perform its traditional missions for state governors, but the bill would have recognized the Guard as "state troops" and no longer as the states' organized militias.[19] The Senate Bill met significant resistance when it hit the House Military Affairs Committee from congressman such as James Hay from Virginia and the Guard's many state adjutants general. The House version of the bill ultimately won out and became the final NDA passed in 1920.

When trying to understand the Guard adjutants general's opposition to the Wadsworth Bill, Palmer consulted his friend New York Guard Major General John O'Ryan, who was a highly respected Guardsman and the only National Guard division commander who retained his command in combat on the Western Front. O'Ryan said that he had discussed the Wadsworth Bill with perhaps "twenty Adjutants General" and found that:

mander-in-Chief, Research Paper, Washington, D.C.: American University Washington College of Law, 2008; S. T. Ansell, "Status of State Militia Under the Hay Bill," *Harvard Law Review*, Vol. 30, No. 7, 1917.

[18] Public Law 66-242, The National Defense Act Amendments of 1920, June 4, 1920.

[19] "Comparative Analysis of House and Senate Bills, Army Reorganization," January 17, 1920, box 4, in the papers of John McAulay Palmer, Washington, D.C.: Library of Congress, 1863–1977.

the majority of them [were] strenuously opposed to any Bill which does not give the National Guard control of itself and does not vest [their authorities as Adjutants General] in the states . . . [and] the power to train [the National Guards in their states] in time of peace.[20]

This rationale of the adjutants general would become a foundational issue for the Guard as it worked over the next 13 years to get Congress to enact legislation that would guarantee its links to the states and to the militia clause of the Constitution.

The measures taken to generate the massive force deemed required to defeat Germany on French battlefields in World War I did not end the debate over the appropriate military policy for the new age. In the years after the passage of the 1920 NDA, Palmer argued for a small but highly trained professional Regular Army complemented by a reserve formed of trained units made up of and led by civilian soldiers. Palmer's idea of having a mass citizen war army led by citizen leaders and not purely Regular Army leaders set him apart from many in the War Department who still favored something along the lines of the 1915 Continental Army plan. Palmer's approach to ensuring the availability and quality of that reserve was to argue for universal military training under federal auspices. Notwithstanding Palmer's influence, a frugal and isolationist Congress was not supportive of large and expensive peacetime militaries. While Palmer wanted several hundred thousand men under the colors, Congress authorized only 140,000 and 180,000 men for the Regular Army and the National Guard, respectively, and rejected universal military training altogether. The Army, seeking to remain "expansible" despite its understrength status, opted to maintain as many Regular and Guard units as possible but kept each at no more than half strength. Organized reserve units consisted only of officers.

Throughout the 1920s and into the 1930s, Palmer maintained influence in military and policy circles by publishing numerous articles and two books on his views on the proper military policy of the United States. In 1930, Palmer published *Washington, Lincoln, Wilson: Three War Statesmen*,[21] in which he claimed to have made an original discovery in the archives of the Library of Congress of George Washington's 1783 *Sentiments on a Peace Establishment*. Palmer then provided his reader a detailed explanation of Washington's plan, concluding, dubiously, that Washington's 1783 proposal was very similar to the military policy Palmer was calling for in the years after World War I.[22] In contrast to his contemporary ideas for military policy, which were,

---

[20] John O'Ryan to John M. Palmer, March 5, 1920, box 5, in the papers of John McAulay Palmer, Washington, D.C.: Library of Congress, 1863–1977.

[21] John McAuley Palmer and John J. Pershing, *Washington, Lincoln, Wilson: Three War Statesmen*, Garden City, N.Y.: Doubleday, Doran & Co., 1930.

[22] For example, Palmer downplayed Washington's belief in the primacy of a professional standing army as the lynchpin to the American security system. Palmer also glossed over Washington's view of the select militia as a federal reserve force only. It is questionable whether Washington in his day would have accepted the militia as a dual reserve component to the Army with statutory allegiance to both state governors and the federal government.

as he argued, the same as Washington's, Palmer castigated Emory Upton as reflecting all the wrongheaded thinking in the current War Department, which he argued was still stuck in an Uptonian malaise of the expansible Regular Army concept. In a sense, Palmer's castigation of Upton and his interpretation of Washington's supposed 1783 plan provided Palmer a historical starting point to argue that his ideas on military policy had been in place since the beginning of the Republic. Palmer argued that if American statesmen in the intervening years had only adopted Washington's plan, the bloody and costly wars America actually fought could have been avoided. Palmer would maintain a strident belief in the correctness of his polemics well into the World War II years and beyond. Palmer's proposals for military policy for the Army were important because of the level of influence he would wield in the years ahead (discussed below) with the highest levels of War Department leadership and its plans for future military policy.

Three years after the publication of *Three War Statesmen*, Congress passed an amendment to the 1916 NDA that is arguably the most important piece of statutory law in the history of the U.S. Army. The 1933 amendment stated that when the National Guard was not federalized for war service, it would be a "reserve component" for the U.S. Army at all times.[23] The amendment stipulated that the Army of the United States shall "consist of the Regular Army, the National Guard of the United States, the National Guard while in the service of the United States, the Officers' Reserve Corps, the Organized Reserves, and the Enlisted Reserve Corps."[24] In effect, the amendment officially tied the Regular Army to the National Guard units of the several states in both times of war and peace, establishing the first complete legal authority for a total army force, because it made the National Guard a reserve component of the Army at all times.

The 1933 amendment also contained a very important change in terminology that reflected increasing reliance on the "raise and support armies" clause to expand the Army by increasing its size in war. The 1916 and 1920 NDAs stipulated that, to federalize the National Guard, Guardsmen had to be drafted for federal service as individuals, thereby "discharging" them from their respective "state militias" duties. The use of the term *draft* in the 1916 and 1920 NDAs was to get around the tricky constitutional issue of employing the federally organized Guard units of the several states under the militia clause of the Constitution for use in foreign wars rather than to suppress internal rebellion or repel invasion. Therefore, the 1933 amendment substituted the word

---

[23] Public Law 73-64, An Act to Amend the National Defense Act of June 3, 1916, June 15, 1933.

[24] U.S. Senate, Committee on Military Affairs, *Amend the National Defense Act*, Senate Report 135, 73rd Congress, 1st Session, Washington, D.C.: U.S. Government Printing Office, 1933; Robert K. Griffith, *Men Wanted for the U.S. Army: America's Experience with an All-Volunteer Army Between the World Wars*, Westport, Conn.: Greenwood Press, 1982.

ordered for the word *drafted*.[25] Accordingly, the law reaffirmed the practice of the post-1916 laws and firmly tied the Guard to the "raise and support armies" clause to ensure that the Guard forces could be deployed overseas.[26]

An indicator of the increasing importance of the "raise and support armies" clause and the declining importance of the militia clause was the change in title in the 1933 amendment from the "Militia Bureau" to the "National Guard Bureau." Indeed, respected military historian Frederick Todd noted in *Military Review* a few years after the law was passed that "at last the attempt to administer the Guard under the 'militia clause' of the Constitution was completely abandoned; today it operates under the 'Army clause.'"[27] Now more than ever, the Guard would be "well regulated," but whereas the Constitutional critics of Washington's day opposed the idea, the National Guard fully endorsed being a part of the Army at all times, its acceptance another manifestation of its continuing embrace of the professionalist mindset. Significantly, the 1933 law's stipulation that the National Guard was a reserve component of the Army at all times—premised on the "raise and support armies" clause—also accepted that, when the Guard was not in federal service and thus under state control, it was still recognized under the Constitution's militia clause. Hence, the 1933 act in effect *joined* the two clauses into law. The 1933 House Committee on Military Affairs report pointed out that the act established a National Guard that had two political masters— the states and the federal government. In stressing the importance of the Guard's dual role of serving as a reserve component of the Army at all times while maintaining its links to the states, the report noted that

> the National Guard of the United States . . . [is] a reserve organization of the Army of the United States, under the Army [armies clause] provisions of the Constitution, leaving the National Guard of the States . . . organized under the militia provisions of the Constitution, intact and unaffected by such amendments.[28]

---

[25] On the "twinning" of the two constitutional clauses, see H. Richard Uviller and William G. Merkel, "The Second Amendment in Context: The Case of the Vanishing Predicate," *Chicago-Kent Law Review*, Vol. 76, January, 2000; Vladeck, 2008; Stephen I. Vladeck, "The Field Theory: Martial Law, the Suspension Power, and the Insurrection Act," *Temple Law Review*, Vol. 80, No. 2, 2007; Richard Allen Epstein, "Executive Power, the Commander in Chief, and the Militia Clause," *Hofstra Law Review Hofstra Law Review*, Vol. 34, No. 2, 2005.

[26] For a clear articulation of the importance difference in terminology between *call*, *draft*, and *order* in U.S. military policy, see Major General Edgar C. Erickson, "Address to the Army War College (February 17, 1954)," in Ellard A. Walsh and Edgar C. Erickson, *The Nation's National Guard*, Washington, D.C.: National Guard Association of the United States, 1954.

[27] Todd, 1941b, p. 170.

[28] U.S. House of Representatives, Committee on Military Affairs, *National Guard Bill*, House Report 141, 73rd Congress, 1st Session, Washington, D.C.: U.S. Government Printing Office, 1933, p. 3. For scholarly arguments on the "twinning" of the two constitutional clauses, see Uviler and Merkel, 2000; Vladeck, 2007; Epstein, 2005.

The irony was that, even though by 1933 the "raise and support armies" clause had eclipsed the militia clause when it came to raising and organizing the Army to fight wars (a sentiment reinforced by the previously mentioned 1917 Supreme Court decision), the 1933 act maintained the militia clause on an equal statutory footing with the "raise and support armies" clause.[29] This elevation of the militia clause also occurred in the face of the fact that, by 1933, the federal government was providing the preponderance of all Guard funding. The federal funding was for the Guard as a reserve component of the Army under the armies clause of the Constitution—but the Guard's association with the militia clause of the Constitution was also central to its institutional identity.

Equally important to the Guard was legal recognition as a *voluntary* reserve for the U.S. Army. As early as 1926, the National Guard Association of the United States (NGAUS) had as its primary political goal for Congress to pass a new law recognizing the National Guard as a voluntary, federal reserve component of the Army at all times.[30] It pushed for this legislation because the Guard had come to fundamentally disagree with the 1920 NDA, which, to federalize the Guard, stipulated that each individual member of the Guard had to be "drafted" into federal service. Guardsmen started to ask why they should be drafted into federal service when they had already made a voluntary commitment to serve when federalized. Two prominent National Guard officers made this argument pointedly to Congress during their consideration of new legislation. Major General Benson Hough of the Ohio National Guard told members of the House Committee on Military Affairs that the current law required individual guardsmen to be "drafted into federal service" and thereby discharged from their duty as state militia. In contrast, the general recommended a bill that would make the National Guard a permanent reserve component to the Army at all times under the armies clause of the Constitution. Doing so would then eliminate the need for individual Guardsmen to be "drafted" into federal service. General Hough went on to note that the bill "will in no way change" a Guardsman's status "as a citizen," nor would it:

> alter his volunteer military obligation to his state and will in no way change his obligation to respond to the call of the President; but will, by his voluntary con-

---

[29] What is interesting is that observers at the time, such as lawyer Frederick Bernays Wiener ("The Militia Clause of the Constitution," *Harvard Law Review*, Vol. 54, No. 2, 1940), and others decades after the act did not see the potential political power of this mechanism. For example, Martha Derthick argued in her 1965 *The National Guard in Politics* that the Guard's power as a political force was waning significantly, to the point where the Guard "would cease to be powerful" as a force in American politics (p. 179).

[30] NGAUS was formed in 1911 from the older National Guard Association that was first established in 1878. The new NGAUS was a more centralized lobbying organization in terms of its shared vision for the National Guard as a dual constitutional reserve to the Army as part of the first line defenses. See Doubler, 2001, p. 138.

sent, prepare the way in advance for his future active Federal service and thus obviate the necessity of subjecting him to the draft without his consent.[31]

Another prominent Guard general, Milton Reckord, who at the time was the Adjutant General of Maryland and during World War I commanded a National Guard infantry regiment in combat, reinforced General Hough's testimony:

> We in the National Guard desire to be a part of the Army of the United States at all times, in peace as well as in war, and yet we also desire to serve in a dual capacity under the militia clause of our respective States. . . . [W]e provide a method by which to create another reserve force similar in every respect to the present Organized Reserves, to be known as the National Guard of the United States; and then . . . we provide, in case of war or emergency declared by Congress, the President may then order this new reserve force into the Federal service . . . under the Army clause, rather than the militia clause.[32]

Thus, the 1933 act gave the Guard exactly what it wanted: dual allegiance to the states and the federal government. Indeed, when the act was discussed on the House Floor on June 5, 1933, Congressman William Patrick Connery, Jr., of Massachusetts stated that "the National Guard has been trying to get this legislation since 1926. Seven years the Guard has favored this type of bill." Connery further noted that "this bill protects the Guard" from the kinds of previous actions by the War Department, such as the Continental Army Plan, and "its passage will greatly help the morale of the Guard."[33]

In 1939, just six years after Congress passed the 1933 act, the United States began to prepare for the possibility of fighting another world war. Congress expanded the Army by increasing manpower authorizations for the Regular Army and the National Guard and in 1940 passed the Selective Service Act, the first peacetime national conscription in the nation's history. Recall that Congress had passed a similar act in April 1917 to increase the size of the Army for World War I; however, that act was passed after the United States declared war on Germany, whereas in 1940, the United States

---

[31] U.S. House of Representatives, *Officers' Reserve Corps—National Guard (Proposed Amendments to the National Defense Act, H.R. 10478: Hearings Before the Committee on Military Affairs)*, Washington, D.C.: U.S. Government Printing Office, 1930.

[32] U.S. House of Representatives, 1930.

[33] 77th Congress, *Congressional Record*, June 5, 1933, pp. 5000–5009; Doubler, 2001, pp. 170–171. The U.S. Houses of Representatives' *National Guard Bill* (House Report No. 141, 1933) states that the origins of the 1933 act came out of the National Guard Association Annual meeting in 1926, hence the congressman's claim that the bill had been "seven years" in the making. For the original rationale by the National Guard for the act, see National Guard Association of the United States, *Annual Convention Report*, Washington, D.C.: National Guard Museum, November 17–19, 1926.

was still at peace and would not declare war on Germany and Japan until December 1941.

Even though establishing a new Selective Service process to increase the size of the Army through conscription was the main thrust of the 1940 law, it also contained a new and profound statement about U.S. military policy. The act declared that:

> . . . in accordance with our [American] traditional military policy as expressed in the National Defense Act of 1916, as amended, that it is essential that the strength and organization of the National Guard, as an integral part of the first-line defenses of this Nation, be at all times maintained and assured.[34]

The notion that there had been a "traditional military policy"—this the first time the phrase appears in statutory law—from the earliest days of the American Republic was largely a fiction created by Palmer. Recall that Palmer's 1930 book *Washington, Lincoln, Wilson: Three War Statesmen* mischaracterized George Washington's 1783 *Sentiments on a Peace Establishment*.[35] Palmer had manipulated Washington's plan, omitting key points and selectively highlighting others, to make it seem like what Washington was calling for in 1783 was exactly the "traditional military policy" stated in the 1940 Selective Service Act. The inclusion of the phrase in the Act was no accident; that same year, Army Chief of Staff George Catlett Marshall had brought Palmer back on to active duty as a Brigadier General to assist Army planners in mobilization planning and eventually in writing postwar military policy. Palmer worked with the writers of the 1940 Selective Service Act to insert the passage on "traditional military policy." Thus Palmer's phrase suggested that there had been one "traditional military policy" for governing the Army and the central role of the National Guard since the Constitution.

Yet what this history has shown is that there was not a neat, clear, and straight line from the Constitution to 1940. Instead, the evolution of military policy was shaped by many factors and lacked the elements of continuity implied by Palmer's invocation of "tradition."[36] Even use of the term *military policy* did not become widespread until after Upton had used the term in the title of his manuscript *The Military Policy of the United States* in the late 1870s. The irony of Palmer's use of the phrase, along with his castigation of Upton and the assertion that Washington's "military policy" was the same as his, was that it was Upton who first coined the term. Hence, the notion of a

---

[34] Public Law 76-783, An Act to Provide for the Common Defense by Increasing the Personnel of the Armed Forces of the United States and Providing for Its Training, September 16, 1940.

[35] Palmer and Pershing, 1930. For a contemporary critical review of Palmer's book, see T. H. Thomas, "*The Biography of the Late Marshal Foch*, by Major-General Sir George Aston," *American Historical Review*, Vol. 35, No. 4, July 1930. For a similar but less harsh critique of Palmer, see Weigley, 1962, p. 237; Kohn, 1975, p. 45.

[36] Wiener, 1940; Todd, 1941b, p. 170; Edward Samuel Corwin, *Total War and the Constitution: Five Lectures on the William W. Cook Foundation at the University of Michigan, March 1946*, New York: Knopf, 1947.

straight line between the "traditional military policy" stated in today's laws that govern the Army all the way back to Washington's 1783 *Sentiments on a Peace Establishment* is a historical fabrication.

Indeed, it is important to note that Congress's passing of the 1933 act reflected its historical period and its unique challenges, which were very different problems than today's military policy has to confront. For example, in 1930, the only way major portions of the National Guard (and officers of the Officer Reserve Corps ordered to active duty) could be ordered into federal service was if Congress declared war or a national emergency. Accordingly, when it came to the day-to-day activities of the state National Guards, the idea behind the 1933 act was that, in times of peace (when not federalized for war or national emergency), the state National Guards would have their "administration, officering [and] training" carried out by the states. In other words, it was black and white: Either there was war or national emergency and the Guard could be mobilized, or there was not and the Guard remained under the control of the states.[37]

But the 1940 Selective Service Act's use of the phrase "traditional military policy" gave the legislation and the policy it charted the feel of a culmination of history, with the implication that after so many years, the United States had finally settled on the right military policy. Indeed, two years after the passing of the 1940 act, Palmer spoke in April 1942 at the annual convention of the Adjutant Generals Association of the United States, asserting that, had Congress in 1920 accepted all his proposals, it would have settled "our military policy forever."[38] But there was nothing in the years from 1903 to 1940 to suggest that the history of U.S. military policy had come to an end, that a plan to settle "forever" U.S. military policy was available to decisionmakers, or that all the historical forces that had shaped U.S military policy over time had culminated in the 1940 act and required no more fundamental changes or adjustments.

So powerful was this perception of an apotheosis in military policy that, in February 1944, only four months before the D-Day invasion of Europe, NGAUS president Major General Ellard Walsh let it be known to the War Department leadership that the Guard would not support any postwar bill on universal military training and military policy unless it contained at the beginning of the bill the proclamation of the "traditional military policy" of the United States that made it essential for "the strength and organization of the National Guard . . . be at all times maintained." Walsh, who at the time was president of the NGAUS, warned that if such language was not included in the bill:

> the National Guard will oppose the . . . Bill and other similar measures until such time as the interests of the sovereign States and the National Guard are secured by

---

[37] U.S. House of Representatives, 1930.

[38] Address of Brigadier General John McAuley Palmer, excerpts from the transcript of the shorthand report of the proceedings of the Adjutants General Association Annual Meeting, April 21, 1942, in the papers of John McAulay Palmer, Washington, D.C.: Library of Congress, 1863–1977.

the inclusion of the protective language contained in the Selective Training and Service Act of 1940.[39]

The idea of continuity in military policy is reflected today in the current version of the fundamental laws that govern the Total Army. For example, Title 32 of U.S. Code—National Guard—states that the Army National Guard "is trained, and has its officers appointed, under the sixteenth [militia] clause of section 8, article I of the Constitution." However, the sentence that immediately follows states that the Army National Guard "is organized, armed, and equipped wholly or partly at Federal expense; and it is federally recognized"— in other words, the organizing, arming, and equipping of the Army National Guard is premised on the armies clause of the Constitution. This language has appeared virtually unchanged in every version of Title 32 dating back to 1934. Of course, the significance of 1934 is that it was the year after the 1933 act joined the two constitutional clauses into statutory law. That the wording in Title 32 has remained unchanged reflects that statutory joining.

---

[39] Ellard A. Walsh, "Ellard Walsh to the Adjutants Generals of the Several States and the Territories and Members of the Executive Committee of the National Guard Conference," *Universal Military Training*, February 19, 1944.

CHAPTER FIVE

From the Korean War to Total Force Policy

Though the fundamental laws that governed the U.S. Army did not change in the years following World War II, refinements and adjustments continued. There were also significant changes in the strategic context, a point brought home above all by the Korean War, which began in 1950. For the first time, the United States needed to be able to quickly deploy large and capable formations. The existing mechanisms to generate new forces or to train and prepare existing ARNGUS and USAR units were too slow for the accelerated timeframe of modern crises. Moreover, President Harry S. Truman decided not to resort to total war and not to mobilize the citizenry to fight the Korean War. This marked an important divergence from the Army's method of expansion up to that point, which represented something of an all-or-nothing approach: The United States either mobilized the citizenry by whatever means or made do with what it had available. Korea called for something in the middle, given that the Regular Army at that time was too small—as was usually the case in American history—to meet policymakers' needs, namely to provide the kind of force needed to fight in Korea while also maintaining a sizable presence in Europe.

What the Army did was work to increase the readiness of USAR and ARNGUS units to shorten the period of time required to get them ready for deployment. This meant, among other things, turning USAR units, which previously had existed on paper only, into more substantive formations. It also meant spending a lot more money and thinking more about the compatibility and integration of RC units into the overall fighting force.[1]

---

[1] Roy Edgar Appleman, *South to the Naktong, North to the Yalu: June–November 1950*, Washington, D.C.: Center of Military History, U.S. Army, 1992, pp. 60–76; Roy K. Flint, "Task Force Smith and the 24th Division: Delay and Withdrawal, 5–19 July 1950," in William Stoft and Charles Heller, eds., *America's First Battles, 1776–1965*, Lawrence, Kan.: Kansas University Press, 1984; Bruce Cumings, *The Korean War: A History*, New York: Modern Library, 2010; William Whitney Stueck, *Rethinking the Korean War: A New Diplomatic and Strategic History*, Princeton, N.J.: Princeton University Press, 2002; David Rees, *Korea: The Limited War*, New York: St. Martin's Press, 1964; John Michael Kendall, *An Inflexible Response: United States Army Manpower Mobilization Policies 1945–1957*, Ann Arbor, Mich.: University of Microfilms International, 1982; Irving Heymont and E. W. McGregor, *Review and Analysis of Recent Mobilizations and Deployments of US Army Reserve Components*, McLean, Va.: Research Analysis Corp., 1972; Leverett Saltonstall, *Status of Reserve and National Guard Forces of the Armed*

In 1964, as the U.S. Army began to look to the likely possibility that it would be sending combat forces to Vietnam, Secretary of Defense Robert McNamara sought to significantly revise this tripartite system. Recognizing the staying power of the set of laws that governed the U.S. Army, McNamara proposed to turn the Army Reserve into a manpower pool and to fold whatever units remained into the National Guard. The Guard had no problem with McNamara's proposal, but the Army Reserve—now backed by a powerful lobbying group of its own called the Reserve Officers Association (ROA)—ultimately persuaded Congress to scrap McNamara's proposal.[2]

The next effort to modify Army force structure without reassessing the fundamental laws governing the Army came in 1972–1974, when the Army was led through the closing years of the Vietnam War by Chief of Staff General Creighton Abrams. To stem post-Vietnam significant force cutting, Abrams argued for placing an increased number of combat and combat support structure in the reserve components to maintain 16 divisions in the Regular Army but within a personnel end strength cap established by Congress of 785,000.[3]

The concept that became known as Army Total Force Policy included making greater investments in Army RC (ARNGUS and USAR) readiness to shorten the amount of mobilization time that RC units required. For example, it meant that the Army needed to purchase new equipment for RC units rather than continuing to rely on used materiel from the Regular Army. Finally, it meant recognizing that many RC units, particularly USAR units, would in practice have to mobilize at the same time, or even before, first-tier Regular Army units because they performed essential support functions. Since the advent of Army Total Force Policy in the early 1970s, the struggle has been to realize the aim of having the right RC units receive the right equipment and the right training as a function of their specific place in operational plans.[4]

Services Report of the Interim Subcommittee on Preparedness of the Committee on Armed Services, Washington, D.C.: Chairman of the Senate Committee on Armed Services, January 29, 1954.

[2] U.S. House of Representatives, *Hearings on Proposed Merger of Army Reserve Components: Hearing Before the Subcommittee No. 2 of the Committee on Armed Services*, Washington, D.C.: U.S. Government Printing Office, March 25, 1965; "'Disgusted' Officers Assert McNamara Bypasses Congress," *New York Times*, December 13, 1964, p. 83; George Fielding Eliot, *Reserve Forces and the Kennedy Strategy*, Harrisburg, Pa.: Stackpole Co., 1962.

[3] U.S. Senate, *Testimony of Assistant Secretary of Defense William Brehm on Defense, Manpower, and Reserve Affairs: Hearing Before the Committee on Armed Service, Subcommittee on Manpower and Personnel*, Washington, D.C.: U.S. Government Printing Office, July 30, 1975, pp. 13–14. The best account of the origins and history of the All-Volunteer Force is Bernard Rostker, *I Want You! The Evolution of the All-Volunteer Force*, Santa Monica, Calif.: RAND Corporation, MG-265-RC, 2006. See also Conrad C. Crane, "The Myth of the Abrams Doctrine," in Jason Warren, ed., *Drawdown: After America's Wars*, New York: New York University Press, forthcoming; J. R. Schlesinger and U.S. Department of Defense Historical Office, *Public Statements of James R. Schlesinger, Secretary of Defense*, Washington, D.C., 1973; Creighton Williams Abrams, *The Sixteen Division Force: Anatomy of a Decision*, thesis, Ft. Leavenworth, Kan.: U.S. Army Command and General Staff College, 1975, pp. 38–39.

[4] Melvin Laird, "Memorandum on Readiness of the Selected Reserve," Washington, D.C.: Office of the Secretary of Defense, August 23, 1970; Patrick Cronin, *The Total Force Policy in Historical Perspective*, Arlington, Va.: Center for Naval Analyses, June 1987.

That struggle remained the centerpiece for the Total Army force into the 1980s and 1990s and, after 9/11, during the Global War on Terror. Indeed during America's post-9/11 wars in Iraq and Afghanistan, the Army has seen the use of all three components to meet rapidly turning rotational demands. Whereas prior to 9/11 only a few ARNGUS and USAR units were deployed overseas in various types of operational missions and training exercises, the GWOT saw both reserve components fully integrated into deployment rotations to take part of operations in Iraq and Afghanistan. The term *operational reserve* came to be during the GWOT era as a way to recognize the important part of current operations played by the Army's two reserve components.

CHAPTER SIX

Conclusion

It is hard to find a "traditional military policy" in this brief history, if that phrase is meant to imply some consistency in the nation's approach to fielding an army over its long history. Rather, the evolution of the Army and the military policy that authorizes, empowers, and governs it can be described in terms of successive compromises between different perspectives and interests, all of which shaped how each generation approached the task of adapting the system they inherited to what they understood to be the requirements of the day. The force mix discussion in today's Army is vastly different from that which took place at the 1787 Constitutional Convention or the congressional debates over the course of the 19th and first half of the 20th centuries.[1] From this, we conclude that history should only be a guide: Given our very different needs today, there is no necessary reason to bind ourselves to the compromises made by previous generations. We also suggest that previous generations did not feel compelled to hold to the compromises of the generations before them. Of course, various parties made use of history in arguing their case, but it was the perceived military requirements and the social, political, and strategic contexts of the time, not the compromises and deals of the past, that drove the determination of solutions.

The easing of the Army's operational tempo after Iraq and Afghanistan means that hard questions are being asked again about what the Army should be. When thinking about the future force, we should free decisionmaking from the pattern of past choices and focus on what the present and future security needs of the nation demand of the Army.

This examination of the past demonstrates the timelessness of the question of what the military policy for the Army should be. What is new—and what must be the critical aspect of the discussion—is the context in which the question is being asked. We need an Army based on a vision of the future that is informed, but not

---

[1] One significant change is the growing emphasis since the 1990s on the use of private military and security companies. See Deborah D. Avant, *The Market for Force: The Consequences of Privatizing Security*, Cambridge, UK: Cambridge University Press, 2005; P. W. Singer, *The Rise of the Privatized Military Industry*, updated ed., Ithaca, N.Y.: Cornell University Press, 2007; Molly Dunigan, *Victory for Hire: Private Security Companies' Impact on Military Effectiveness*, Stanford, Calif.: Stanford University Press, 2011; Bruce Stanley, *Outsourcing Security: Private Military Contractors and U.S. Foreign Policy*, Potomac, Md.: Potomac Books, 2015.

constrained, by the past. It might be the case that the answers to these questions point to an Army that looks a lot like what exists today, with a tripartite force structure of a Regular Army, Army National Guard, and U.S. Army Reserve. But that conclusion should be based on analysis of present and future needs rather than the presumption of immutability.

Indeed, the current system is strikingly different from anything the Framers of the Constitution imagined. Once considered anathema, the United States now largely entrusts its national security to a standing, professional force—its Regular Army. To augment its regular forces, the Army has two professionalized standing reserve components that are resourced and organized under the "raise and support armies" clause of the Constitution. Once organized to defend a growing nation protected by two oceans, the Army can now deploy globally and fight decisively on very short notice. Accordingly, the relative reliance on the two constitutional clauses that are the legal basis for the Army—the "raise and support armies" clause and the militia clause—has evolved with the growth of the nation and its dynamic security needs. That evolution has seen an increasing importance of Congress's use of the armies clause to organize, train, equip, and expand the Army. There has been a concomitant decline in the importance of the militia clause, which no longer serves as a principal statutory foundation for how Congress organizes and equips the Army.

Accordingly, the Supreme Court, when rendering decisions on the laws that govern the Army, has consistently ruled that the "raise and support armies" clause is plenary and supreme.[2] To be sure, the Constitution has not changed. The "raise and support armies" clause and the militia clause are still on the books. Yet there has been a slow, sporadic, and crisis-driven evolution away from reliance on the militia clause toward the "raise and support armies" clause. Over time, the state National Guards have traded autonomy for federal funding, to the point where it is now fully funded, organized, and equipped by the federal government. In return, the National Guards

---

[2] For a Supreme Court ruling on the relative importance of the two clauses when it comes to organizing and training the Army for war and conflict, see Justice John Paul Stevens' ruling in *Perpich v. Department of Defense*, 496 U.S. 334 (1990). This case was based on the Governor of Minnesota Rudy Perpich's objection to the federal government's deployment of members of the Minnesota National Guard under federal status to carry out a summer training mission in Central America. Perpich argued that he was unable to withhold his consent and prevent the Minnesota Guard from carrying out this training, thereby violating the militia clause of the Constitution, which states that the militia when not under federal control falls under the authority of State governors. Justice Stevens, speaking for a unanimous court, upheld the Department of Defense's right to deploy the Minnesota Guard for summer training in Central America. He argued "the Congressional power to call forth the militia may in appropriate cases supplement its broader power to raise armies and provide for the common defense and general welfare, but it does not limit those powers." Also see the 1933 House Committee on Military Affairs report on the National Guard Bill, which clearly saw the armies clause of the Constitution as supreme when dealing with matters pertaining to the organization, training, and preparations for the Army to fight wars. The report argued that when it comes to defending the nation and building and Army "the federal obligation . . . is paramount to the State obligation, and when the two conflict, that of the Federal becomes primary and superior" (U.S. House of Representatives, Committee on Military Affairs, 1933).

of the several states, while over-armed for natural disasters and civil disturbances, are a reserve component of the Army at all times.

One would be mistaken, however, to take from this legislative evolution the thought that the militia clause has ceased to be relevant. It remains the legal basis for the National Guard's peacetime relationship to the states. The existence of a state-based organization across 54 states and territories creates a level of political clout that belies the Guard's reliance on federal funding. We can see that clout behind the authority Major General Ellard Walsh, president of the NGAUS, marshaled in opposing post–World War II plans for universal military training unless policymakers maintained the strength and organization of the National Guard. And, of course, we see it in today's debate on the political wisdom of the Army's Aviation Restructure Initiative and, for that matter, the Air Force's decision to remove from its inventory the A-10, an aircraft deployed solely with the Air National Guard.

Tensions between the Guard and the Department of the Army and the Office of Secretary of Defense brought into existence the National Commission on the Future of the Army, which in turn highlights the importance of this study on "traditional" military policy. That policy may be impossible to find, but whatever it is at any given time, it will be the outcome of competing political forces, lodged ultimately in the twin clauses of the Constitution, and deeply imbedded in the nation's history and political culture. It will almost surely not be analytically perfect, the result of careful systems analysis of competing alternatives. As such, it will make no one completely happy. But that has not prevented the nation from coming up with useful policies when the need arose. Perhaps that is especially the case today, when the current regime of fundamental laws that authorize, empower, and govern the Army were written for a nation between 1903 and 1940 that confronted a vastly different security environment than what confronts the United States today.

Legislation Pertaining to the Evolution of U.S. Military Policy

Table A.1
Legislative Acts Pertaining to the Evolution of U.S. Military Policy

Statute/Act	Historical Context	Significance	Links to Titles 10 and 32
U.S. Constitution: Militia, Raise/Support Armies, and President as Commander in Chief Clauses	• 1787: Framers want small standing army • Framers envision a select portion of the militia as a federal reserve • Framers also envision the militia as the military force to deal with domestic issues such as insurrection and enforcement of laws	• The constitutional basis for Regular Army, federal army reserve, and militias • No constitutional link between Regular Army and militia • Future policy—laws enacted—would therefore define roles of militia and Regular Army	• Title 32 states National Guard is trained and has its officers appointed under militia clause • Title 10 organized current U.S. Army Total Force under raise/support clause
1792 Militia Act	• George Washington wants militia organized on his 1783 Sentiments on a Peace Establishment	• Congress passes militia law with no mechanism for federal enforcement • Is based on militia clause of Constitution • Only militia law until 1903	• Title 32 acknowledges 1792 act and that National Guard is organized under the militia clauses of the Constitution
1795 Amendment to 1792 Calling Forth Act	• Concern over 1794 Whiskey Rebellion and possible future rebellions • Congress's trust in Washington leads to Congress authorizing executive control over militia to deal with domestic problems	• Gives President power to call forth militia without restrictions placed by the 1792 act • Starts the statutory movement away from the militia envisioned in Constitution	• Title 10 gives president authority to either "call forth" or "order" National Guard without congressional authorization per 1795 act
1799 "Augment the Army" Act	• Failure of negotiations with France increased fear of war between the two nations • Domestic unrest at home over taxes to pay for military mobilization increases need for expanded military to deal with insurrections	• Gives President power to expand temporarily the Regular Army by 24 regiments • President given authority to accept organized companies of volunteers from the militia into federal service • 1799 act gives President authority to use this expanded Army for the same purposes when "calling forth" the militia	• Title 10 gives President power to expand Regular Army and use it for domestic problems in combination with National Guard per the 1795 act

Table A.1—Continued

Statute/Act	Historical Context	Significance	Links to Titles 10 and 32
1807 Insurrection Act	• With frontier expanding and continuing domestic unrest, there is need for Regular Army for internal problems in addition to militias	• Gives President authority to use the Regular Army and navy for internal rebellions and other problems • Completes the statutory movement away from militia envisioned in Constitution	• Title 10 gives President authority to use Regular Army for domestic problems in combination with National Guard
1863 Enrollment Act	• American Civil War. Union Army having trouble relying on states to bring men and units to under federal control to meet manpower demand after two years of war with high casualties	• First federal statutory law that authorized a federal draft premised on universal military duty under the "raise and support armies" clause	• Title 10 relies on the Constitution to give it the statutory means to raise and support an army • Implicit is the assumption that a national draft might be necessary to do so, as stipulated in Title 50
1898 Act to Provide for Temporarily Increasing the Peace Establishment of the United States in Time of War	• Spanish-American War: Both Regular Army and National Guard unprepared for expeditionary warfare • Debacle of deploying the Army to Cuba to fight Spain spurs significant postwar Army reforms	• Continues Congress on path increasing reliance on armies clause to organized army for war and maintains precedent for American men liable for service in "national forces"	• Same as 1863 Enrollment Act
1903 Act to Promote Efficiency of Militia (Dick Act)	• Spanish-American War reveals problems expanding Army and readiness of army and state militias (now, National Guard) • Secretary of War (Elihu Root) implements major reforms for U.S. Army • U.S. enters world stage as new global power • Perceived need for major Army reform to fight 20th century industrial wars	• First update to Militia Act for federal organizing of militia since 1792 act • Is based on militia clause • Is statutory birthday of modern Guard • Gives federal recognition of Guard as "organized militia" • Directs Guard to organize like Regular Army • Establishes federal oversight • Formalizes process of trading autonomy for federal aid • Direct Guard units to train 24 drill periods a year and 5-day summer encampment • Funds Guard 5-day encampment	• Title 32 refers to Guard as "organized militia" and directs Guard to be organized like Regular Army • Title 32 is premised on militia and armies clauses of Constitution

Table A.1—Continued

Statute/Act	Historical Context	Significance	Links to Titles 10 and 32
1908 Army Medical Reserve Act (April)	• Experience In Spanish-American War with casualties because of poor sanitation and health issues drives need for reform in Army medical care	• Establishes Medical Reserve Corp of doctors • Statutory birthday of Army Reserve	• Title 10 Army Reserves premised on armies clause
1908 Dick Act Amendment	• Growing tension between Regular Army and War Department and National Guard • Constitutional debate over use of Guard in foreign wars as organized militia • Guard worries federal volunteers will eclipse its desire to be in first line of defense	• Establishes National Guard as Organized Militia of Several States when called to federal service before any volunteers (individuals or units) and can deploy overseas • Further stokes legal debate over constitutionality of deploying the Guard, organized on the militia clause, outside of United States	• Title 32 stipulates National Guard is trained and has its officers appointed under the militia clause
1916 NDA	• World War I underway for two years • Mexican border issues • Debate over whether to have federal-only reserve or National Guard as reserve in first line of defense • Need to reorganize Army for industrial-age warfare • Preparedness movement led by Elihu Root and other leading progressives argues for centralization of Army, universal military training for all American adult males, and rejection of Guard as reserve force to Army, and calls for federal reserve force envisioned in the War Department's "Continental Army Plan"	• Establishes National Guard as component of Army when federalized and in service of U.S. • Constitutional premise is Armies clause • Directs Guard to organize as Regular Army • Gives detailed organization direction for Army. • Establishes Organized Reserves and Reserve Officers Training Corps (ROTC) • Funds Guard for weekly armory training • Is major increase of federal oversight and control of Guard • Sets end strength goal for guard at 435,000 and Regular Army at 280,000 • States that Guard when federalized will be drafted as individual • Establishes Militia Bureau under Secretary of War, not Army Chief of Staff	• Title 10 recognizes Guard as a component of the Army when federalized • Virtually all funding for National Guard under Title 10 is based on Congress organizing the Guard for war under the armies clause • Title 10 allows for ROTC

Table A.1—Continued

Statute/Act	Historical Context	Significance	Links to Titles 10 and 32
1917 Selective Service Act	• U.S. enters World War I, needs to form quickly a mass citizen-based war army. • Selective Service national draft is the means to provide manpower.	• First major national draft in American history • Draws on 1898 Act and 1863 Enrollment Act that virtually all adult males are susceptible to federal military service • First time Army receives major amounts of manpower without using the state militia systems	• Title 10 is statutory framework to carry out constitutional provision to raise and support armies • National conscription is an implicit mechanism in Title 10 and explicitly stated in Title 50 to carry out that function, if needed • Conscription into federal forces premised on armies clause
1920 Amendment to 1916 NDA	• End of World War I yields more debate on how to organize peacetime army • War Department produces plan similar to 1915 Continental Army Plan that calls for federal-only reserve to Army • Backlash from Congress • John M. Palmer becomes key advisor to Senate Military Affairs Committee • Demobilization of Guard as individuals not units embitters Guard toward Regular Army	• Continues much of 1916 NDA • Sets end strength goal for Guard 435,000, Regular Army 280,000 (but over next 20 years neither is funded to those levels) • Word "draft" used to bring Guard to federal service but says Guard can be used for any mission (implying foreign wars) • Makes Chief of Militia a Guard officer (formerly a Regular Army officer); also says if Guard demobilized from federal service will be by units, not individuals	• Title 10 National Guard Bureau headed by Guard officer

Table A.1—Continued

Statute/Act	Historical Context	Significance	Links to Titles 10 and 32
1933 Amendment to 1916 NDA	• Main problem is how to mobilize mass citizen-based war army • Both Regular Army and Guard at 50% • Organized Reserves units are manned at skeleton levels • Based on WWI experience NGAUS and Guard lobby Congress hard for Guard to be made reserve component of Army at all times • National Guard had sought this kind of legislation since the years following end of World War I	• Is statutory birth of modern guard as dual state and federal reserve force • Establishes U.S. Army as the Regular Army, the National Guard of the United States, the National Guard while in the service of the United States, the Officers' Reserve Corps, the Organized Reserves, and the Enlisted Reserve Corps • Says Guard is reserve component of US Army at all times; because Guard is permanent reserve of Army, the word "ordered" is used for first time • The statutory birthday of the modern Army Total Force	• Title 10 defines U.S. Army as Regular Army, Army National Guard of the United States, the Army National Guard while in the Service of the United States, and the Army Reserve • Title 10 uses "call forth" and "order" to federalize Guard • Joins the armies and militia clauses into statutory law • Title 32 reflects "joining" by stating Guard is trained and has officers appointed under militia clause; however, it is organized and equipped under the armies clause
1940 Selective Service Act	• World War II looms • Regular Army, Guard and Organized Reserves mobilizing and preparing • Palmer brought back by Marshal to think about postwar military policy • Guard worries again about being eclipsed by War Department relying on Army Reserve before Guard	• Stipulates explicitly the term "traditional military policy of the United States" is to maintain "at all times" the National Guard as "integral part of first line defenses"	• Title 32 (as does Title 50) stipulates almost verbatim the term "traditional military policy" as stated in the 1940 Selective Service Act

Lists of Figures and Tables

Figure

Tables

Abbreviations

armies clause or "raise and support armies" clause	Article 1, Section 8, Clause 12 of the Constitution, which grants Congress the power "to raise and support Armies, but no Appropriation of Money to that Use shall be for a longer Term than two Years"
ARNGUS	Army National Guard of the United States
GWOT	Global War on Terror
militia clause	Article 1, Section 8, Clauses 15 and 16 of the Constitution, which grant Congress the power "to provide for calling forth the Militia to execute the Laws of the Union, suppress Insurrections and repel Invasions" and "to provide for organizing, arming, and disciplining, the Militia, and for governing such Part of them as may be employed in the Service of the United States, reserving to the States respectively, the Appointment of the Officers, and the Authority of training the Militia according to the discipline prescribed by Congress"
NCFA	National Commission on the Future of the Army
NDA	National Defense Act
NGAUS	National Guard Association of the United States
RC	reserve component
USAR	U.S. Army Reserve

References

77th Congress, *Congressional Record*, June 5, 1933.

"A Brief History of the Oldest Minnesota National Guard Company," *National Guardsman*, May 1901.

Abrams, Creighton Williams, *The Sixteen Division Force: Anatomy of a Decision*, thesis, Ft. Leavenworth, Kan.: U.S. Army Command and General Staff College, 1975.

Adams, Willi Paul, *The First American Constitutions: Republican Ideology and the Making of the State Constitutions in the Revolutionary Era*, Lanham, Md.: Rowman & Littlefield Publishers, 2001.

Anderson, Fred, *A People's Army: Massachusetts Soldiers and Society in the Seven Years' War*, Chapel Hill, N.C.: University of North Carolina Press, 1984.

Anderson, Fred, *Crucible of War: The Seven Years' War and the Fate of Empire in British North America, 1754–1766*, New York: Alfred A. Knopf, 2000.

Annals of Congress, Washington, D.C.: Library of Congress, various years.

Anonymous, "The Federalist Farmer No. XVIII," in Herbert J. Storing, ed., *The Complete Anti-Federalist*, Chicago: University of Chicago Press, 1788, pp. 339–349.

Ansell, S. T., "Status of State Militia Under the Hay Bill," *Harvard Law Review*, Vol. 30, No. 7, 1917, pp. 712–723.

Appleman, Roy Edgar, *South to the Naktong, North to the Yalu: June–November 1950*, Washington, D.C.: Center of Military History, U.S. Army, 1992.

Arver v. United States, 245 U. S. 366, 386 (December 1918).

Avant, Deborah D., *The Market for Force: The Consequences of Privatizing Security*, Cambridge, UK: Cambridge University Press, 2005.

Bahar, Michael, "The Presidential Intervention Principle: The Domestic Use of the Military and the Power of the Several States," *Harvard National Security Journal*, Vol. 5, No. 2, 2014.

Bailey, Kenneth Roy, *A Search for Identity: The West Virginia National Guard, 1877–1921*, dissertation, Ohio State University, 1976.

Bailyn, Bernard, *The Ideological Origins of the American Revolution*, Cambridge, Mass.: Belknap Press, 1967.

Barnett, Randy E., "Was the Right to Keep and Bear Arms Conditioned on Service in an Organized Militia?" *Texas Law Review*, Vol. 83, 2004.

Barron, David J., and Martin S. Ledermen, "The Commander in Chief at the Lowest Ebb: A Constitutional History," *Harvard Law Review*, Vol. 121, No. 4, February 2008.

Barry, Herbert, "In What Way Can the National Guard Be Modified So as to Make It an Effective Reserve to the Regular Army in Both War and Peace?" *Journal of Military Service Institution of the United States*, Vol. 39, July–December 1906.

Bauer, K. Jack, "The Battles on the Rio Grande: Palo Alto and Resaca de la Palma, 8–9 May 1846," in William Stoft and Charles Heller, eds., *1776–1965, America's First Battles*, Lawrence, Kan.: Kansas University Press, 1984.

Bauer, K. Jack, and H. Sutton James, Jr., *The Mexican War, 1846–1848*, New York: Macmillan, 1974.

Beckett, Ian, *Britain's Part-Time Soldiers: The Amateur Military Tradition, 1558–1945*, Barnsley, UK: Pen & Sword, 2011.

Bernardo, C. Joseph, and Eugene Hayward Bacon, *American Military Policy, Its Development Since 1775*, Harrisburg, Pa.: Military Service Pub. Co., 1955.

Bernstein, Iver, *The New York City Draft Riots: Their Significance for American Society and Politics in the Age of the Civil War*, Oxford, UK: Oxford University Press, 1990.

Boies, Henry Martyn, "Our National Guard," *Harper's New Monthly Magazine*, 1880, pp. 915–922.

Cantor, Louis, *The Creation of the Modern National Guard: The Dick Militia Act of 1903*, PhD dissertation, Durham, N.C.: Duke University, 1963.

Carney, Stephen A., *Guns Along the Rio Grande Palo Alto and Resaca de la Palma*, Washington, D.C.: U.S. Army Center of Military History, 2005.

Carter, William H., "When Diplomacy Fails," *The North American Review*, Vol. 187, No. 626, 1908, pp. 23–33.

Carter, William Harding, and James Wolcott Wadsworth, Jr., "Creation of the American General Staff, Personal Narrative of the General Staff System of the American Army, by Major General William Harding Carter, Presented by Mr. Wadsworth, January 22, 1924—Referred to the Committee on Printing," 1924.

Coakley, Robert, *Federal Use of Militia and the National Guard in Civil Disturbances*, Washington, D.C.: Brookings Institution, 1941.

———, *The Role of Federal Military Forces in Domestic Disorders, 1789–1878*, Washington, D.C.: U.S. Army Center of Military History, 1989.

Colby, Elbridge "The Status of the National Guard," *Central Law Journal*, January 1925.

Cooper, Jerry, "National Guard Reform, The Army, and the Spanish-American War: The View from Wisconsin," *Military Affairs*, Vol. 42, No. 1, January 1978.

———, *The Militia and National Guard in America Since Colonial Times: A Reference Guide*, Westport, Conn.: Greenwood Press, 1993.

———, *The Rise of the National Guard: The Evolution of the American Militia, 1865–1920*, Lincoln: University of Nebraska Press, 1997.

Cooper, Jerry M., *The Army and Civil Disorder: Federal Military Intervention in Labor Disputes, 1877–1900*, PhD dissertation, Madison, Wis.: University of Wisconsin, 1971.

———, *The Rise of the National Guard: The Evolution of the American Militia, 1865–1920*, Lincoln: University of Nebraska Press, 1998.

Corwin, Edward Samuel, *Total War and the Constitution: Five Lectures on the William W. Cook Foundation at the University of Michigan, March 1946*, New York: Knopf, 1947.

Cosmas, Graham A., *An Army for Empire: The United States Army in the Spanish-American War*, Columbia, Mo.: University of Missouri Press, 1971.

Coulter, E. Merton, and Frank L. Owsley, "The Confederate States of America, 1861–1865," *The Journal of Economic History*, Vol. 10, No. 2, 1950, pp. 230–231.

Crane, Conrad C., "*The Myth of the Abrams Doctrine*," in Jason Warren, ed., *Drawdown: After America's Wars*, New York: New York University Press, forthcoming.

Cronin, Patrick, *The Total Force Policy in Historical Perspective*, Arlington, Va.: Center for Naval Analyses, June 1987.

Crossland, Richard B., and James T. Currie, *Twice the Citizen: A History of the United States Army Reserve, 1908–1983*, Washington, D.C.: Office of the Chief, Army Reserve, 1984.

Cumings, Bruce, *The Korean War: A History*, New York: Modern Library, 2010.

Cunliffe, Marcus, *Soldiers & Civilians: The Martial Spirit in America, 1775–1865*, Boston: Little, Brown, 1968.

Currie, David P., *The Constitution in Congress: The Federalist Period, 1789–1801*, Chicago: University of Chicago Press, 1999.

"The Debate over National Military Institutions: An Issue Slowly Resolved, 1775–1815," in William M. Fowler, Jr., and Wallace Coyle, eds., *The American Revolution: Changing Perspectives*, Boston: Northeastern, 1979.

The Debates and Proceedings in the Congress of the United States, Thirteenth Congress, Third Session, Washington, D.C.: U.S. Government Printing Office, 1814.

Derthick, Martha, *The National Guard in Politics*, Cambridge, Mass.: Harvard University Press, 1965.

Deutrich, Mabel E., *Struggle for Supremacy: The Career of General Fred C. Ainsworth*, Washington, D.C.: Public Affairs Press, 1962.

"'Disgusted' Officers Assert McNamara Bypasses Congress," *New York Times*, December 13, 1964, p. 83.

Doubler, Michael D., *I Am the Guard: A History of the Army National Guard, 1636–2000*, Washington, D.C.: Army National Guard, 2001.

Dunigan, Molly, *Victory for Hire: Private Security Companies' Impact on Military Effectiveness*, Stanford, Calif.: Stanford University Press, 2011.

Echevarria, Antulio J., *Reconsidering the American Way of War: U.S. Military Practice from the Revolution to Afghanistan*, Washington, D.C.: Georgetown University Press, 2014.

Ekirch, Arthur A., Jr., *The Civilian and the Military: A History of the American Anti-Militarist Tradition*, Oakland, Calif.: Independent Institute, 2010.

Eliot, George Fielding, *Reserve Forces and the Kennedy Strategy*, Harrisburg, Pa.: Stackpole Co., 1962.

Engdahl, David E., "Soldiers, Riots, and Revolutions: The Law and History of Military Troops in Civil Disorders," *Iowa Law Review*, Vol. 57, No. 1, October 1971, p. 73.

Epstein, Richard Allen, "Executive Power, the Commander in Chief, and the Militia Clause," *Hofstra Law Review Hofstra Law Review*, Vol. 34, No. 2, 2005, pp. 317–328.

Erickson, Edgar C., "Address to the Army War College (February 17, 1954)," in Ellard A. Walsh and Edgar C. Erickson, *The Nation's National Guard*, Washington, D.C.: National Guard Association of the United States, 1954.

Finnegan, John Patrick, *Against the Specter of a Dragon; the Campaign for American Military Preparedness, 1914–1917*, Westport, Conn.: Greenwood Press, 1974.

Flint, Roy K., "Task Force Smith and the 24th Division: Delay and Withdrawal, 5–19 July 1950," in William Stoft and Charles Heller, eds., *America's First Battles, 1776–1965*, Lawrence, Kan.: Kansas University Press, 1984.

Foner, Jack D., *The United States Soldier Between Two Wars: Army Life and Reforms, 1865–1898*, New York: Humanities Press, 1970.

Fowles, Brian Dexter, *A Guard in Peace and War: The History of the Kansas National Guard, 1854–1987*, Manhattan, Kan.: Sunflower University, 1989.

Galloway, Eilene Marie Slack, *History of United States Military Policy on Reserve Forces, 1775–1957*, Washington, D.C.: U.S. Government Printing Office, 1957.

Geary, James W., *We Need Men: The Union Draft in the Civil War*, DeKalb, Ill.: Northern Illinois University Press, 1991.

General Staff, U.S. Department of War, *Report on the Organization of the Land Forces of the United States*, Washington, D.C.: U.S. Government Printing Office, 1912.

Glatthaar, Joseph T., *General Lee's Army: From Victory to Collapse*, New York: Free Press, 2008.

Grant, Ulysses S., *Personal Memoirs*, New York: The Modern Library, 1885.

Grenier, John, *The First Way of War: American War Making on the Frontier, 1607–1814*, Cambridge, UK: Cambridge University Press, 2005.

Griffith, Robert K., *Men Wanted for the U.S. Army: America's Experience with an All-Volunteer Army Between the World Wars*, Westport, Conn.: Greenwood Press, 1982.

Gruber, Ira, "The Anglo-American Military Tradition and the War for American Independence," in Kenneth J. Hagan and William R. Roberts, eds., *Against All Enemies: Interpretations of American Military History from Colonial Times to the Present*, Westport, Conn.: Greenwood Press, 1986.

Hamilton, Alexander, *Continental Congress Report on a Military Establishment*, Washington, D.C.: June 18, 1783.

Harris, William C., *Leroy Pope Walker: Confederate Secretary of War*, Tuscaloosa, Ala.: Confederate Pub. Co., 1962.

Hesseltine, William Best, *Lincoln and the War Governors*, New York: A. A. Knopf, 1948.

Hewes, James E., *From Root to McNamara: Army Organization and Administration, 1900–1963*, Washington, D.C.: Center of Military History, U.S. Army, 1975.

Heymont, Irving, and E. W. McGregor, *Review and Analysis of Recent Mobilizations and Deployments of US Army Reserve Components*, McLean, Va.: Research Analysis Corp., 1972.

Higginbotham, Don, *The War of American Independence; Military Attitudes, Policies, and Practice, 1763–1789*, New York: Macmillan, 1971.

———, "The Federalized Militia Debate: A Neglected Aspect of Second Amendment Scholarship," *The William and Mary Quarterly*, Vol. 55, No. 1, January 1998, p. 20.

Hill, Jim Dan, *The Minute Man in Peace and War: A History of the National Guard*, Harrisburg, Pa.: Stackpole Books, 1964.

Hirsch, Alan, "The Militia Clauses of the Constitution and the National Guard," *University of Cincinnati Law Review*, No. 56, 1988.

Holley, I. B., and John McAuley Palmer, *General John M. Palmer, Citizen Soldiers, and the Army of a Democracy*, Westport, Conn.: Greenwood Press, 1982.

Holmes, Joseph John, *The National Guard of Pennsylvania: Policeman of Industry, 1865–1905*, PhD dissertation, Storrs, Conn.: University of Connecticut, 1971.

House, Jonathan M., "John McAuley Palmer and the Reserve Components," *Parameters*, Vol. 12, No. 3, 1982.

Howard, Michael, "The Use and Abuse of History," *The Royal United Services Institute (RUSI) Journal*, Vol. 138, No. 1, 1993.

Huidekoper, Frederic Louis, and William H. Taft, *Is the United States Prepared for War?* New York: North American Review Pub. Co., 1907.

Interstate National Guard Association, *Fourth Annual Convention*, Washington, D.C., January 20–22, 1902, Washington, D.C.: National Guard Museum.

Jessup, Phillip, *Elihu Root*, two volumes, New York: Dodd Mead, 1938.

Johannsson, Robert, *To the Halls of the Montezuma: The Mexican War in the American Imagination*, New York: Oxford University Press, 1974.

Kendall, John Michael, *An Inflexible Response: United States Army Manpower Mobilization Policies 1945–1957*, Ann Arbor, Mich.: University of Microfilms International, 1982.

Knox, Henry, *A Plan for the General Arrangement of the Militia of the United States*, New York, March 28, 1786.

Kohn, Richard H., *Eagle and Sword: Federalists and the Creation of the Military Establishment in America, 1783–1802*, New York: Free Press, 1975.

———, "The Murder of the Militia System in the Aftermath of the American Revolution," in Stanley J. Underdal, ed., *Military History of the American Revolution: The Proceedings of the 6th Military History Symposium United States Air Force Academy 10–11 October 1974*, Washington, D.C.: U.S. Government Printing Office, 1976.

———, *The United States Military Under the Constitution of the United States, 1789–1989*, New York: New York University Press, 1991.

Kreidberg, Marvin A., and Merton G. Henry, *History of Military Mobilization in the United States Army, 1775–1945*, Washington, D.C.: Department of the Army, 1955.

Laird, Melvin, "Memorandum on Readiness of the Selected Reserve," Washington, D.C.: Office of the Secretary of Defense, August 23, 1970.

Leach, Jack Franklin, *Conscription in the United States: Historical Background*, Rutland, Vt.: C. E. Tuttle Pub. Co., 1952.

Lee, Henry, *The Militia of the United States: What It Has Been, What It Should Be*, Boston: Marvin & Son, 1864.

Lee, Wayne E., *Barbarians and Brothers: Anglo-American Warfare, 1500–1865*, Oxford, UK: Oxford University Press, 2011.

Lender, Mark Edward, "The Social Structure of the New Jersey Brigade: The Continental Line as an American Standing Army," in Peter Karsten, ed., *The Military in America: From the Colonial Era to the Present*, New York: Free Press, 1980.

Levy, Leonard W., *Jefferson & Civil Liberties: The Darker Side*, revised ed., New York: Quadrangle, 1973.

Linderman, Gerald F., *The Mirror of War: American Society and the Spanish-American War*, Ann Arbor, Mich.: University of Michigan Press, 1974.

Linn, Brian, "The American Way of War Revisited," *The Journal of Military History*, Vol. 66, April 2002.

———, *The Echo of Battle: The Army's Way of War*, Cambridge, Mass.: Harvard University Press, 2010.

Logan, John Alexander, and Cornelius Ambrose Logan, *The Volunteer Soldier of America*, Chicago and New York: R. S. Peale & Co., 1887.

Mahon, John K., *The Citizen Soldier in National Defense, 1789–1815*, PhD dissertation, Los Angeles: University of California at Los Angeles, 1950.

———, "A Board of Officers Considers the Condition of the Militia in 1826," *Military Affairs*, Vol. 15, No. 2, 1951.

———, *History of the Militia and the National Guard*, New York; London: Collier Macmillan, 1983.

———, *History of the Second Seminole War, 1835–1842*, Gainesville, Fla.: University Press of Florida, 1985.

Mahon, Robert, *The American Militia: Decade of Decision, 1789–1800*, Gainesville, Fla.: University Press of Florida, 1960.

Maier, Pauline, *Ratification: The People Debate the Constitution, 1787–1788*, New York: Simon and Schuster, 2011.

Marcus, Richard Henry, *The Militia of Colonial Connecticut, 1639–1775*, PhD dissertation, Boulder, Colo.: University of Colorado, 1965.

Mazzone, Jason, "The Commander in Chief," *Notre Dame Law Review*, Vol. 83, 2007–2008.

"Militia and Army: The Secretary of War Favors Closer Relations," *Washington Post*, December 1, 1902.

Millett, Allan R., Peter Maslowski, and William B. Feis, *For the Common Defense: A Military History of the United States from 1607–2012*, New York: Free Press, 2012.

Moore, Albert Burton, *Conscription and Conflict in the Confederacy*, New York: The Macmillan Company, 1924.

Murdock, Eugene C., *Patriotism Limited, 1862–1865: The Civil War Draft and the Bounty System*, Kent, Ohio: Kent State University Press, 1967.

National Commission on the Future of the Army, *Report to the President and to Congress*, Arlington, Va., January 28, 2016.

National Guard Association of the United States, *Annual Convention Report*, Washington, D.C.: National Guard Museum, November 17–19, 1926.

Nenninger, Timothy K., *The Leavenworth Schools and the Old Army: Education, Professionalism, and the Officer Corps of the United States Army, 1881–1918*, Westport, Conn.: Greenwood Press, 1978.

Nevins, Allan, *The War for the Union: War Becomes Revolution, 1862–1863, Volume I*, New York: Scribner, 1959.

Office of Attorney General, Vol. 29, 1912.

Official Report of the Proceedings and Debates of the Third Constitutional Convention of Ohio Assembled in the City of Columbus on Tuesday May 13, 1873, Cleveland, Ohio: W.S. Robison & Company, 1874.

Palmer, John McAulay, collected papers, Washington, D.C.: Library of Congress, 1863–1977.

Palmer, John McAuley, and John J. Pershing, *Washington, Lincoln, Wilson: Three War Statesmen*, Garden City, N.Y.: Doubleday, Doran & Co., 1930.

Pappas, George S., *Prudens Futuri: The US Army War College, 1901–1967*, Carlisle Barracks, Pa.: Alumni Association of the U.S. Army War College, 1967.

Perpich v. Department of Defense, 496 U.S. 334 (1990).

Pettit, James S., "How Far Does Democracy Affect the Organization of Our Armies, and How Can Its Influence Be Most Effectually Utilized?" *Journal of the Military Service Institute of the United States*, No. 38, January–February 1906.

Pisney, Raymond F., *The Brandywine Rangers in the War of 1812*, Wilmington, Del.: Hagley Museum & Library, 1950.

Prakash, Saikrishna Bangalore, *Imperial from the Beginning: The Constitution of the Original Executive*, New Haven, Conn.: Yale University Press, 2015.

Pratt, William D., *A History of the National Guard of Indiana: From the Beginning of the Militia System in 1787 to the Present Time, Including the Services of Indiana Troops in the War with Spain*, Indianapolis, Ind.: W. D. Pratt, Printer and Binder, 1901.

Public Law 64-85, An Act for Making Further and More Effectual Provision for the National Defense, and for Other Purposes, June 3, 1916.

Public Law 65-12, An Act to Authorize the President to Increase Temporarily the Military Establishment of the United States, May 18, 1917.

Public Law 66-242, The National Defense Act Amendments of 1920, June 4, 1920.

Public Law 73-64, An Act to Amend the National Defense Act of June 3, 1916, June 15, 1933.

Public Law 76-783, An Act to Provide for the Common Defense by Increasing the Personnel of the Armed Forces of the United States and Providing for Its Training, September 16, 1940.

Rakove, Jack N., *Original Meanings: Politics and Ideas in the Making of the Constitution*, New York: Vintage Books, 1997.

Rees, David, *Korea: The Limited War*, New York: St. Martin's Press, 1964.

Rich, Bennett Milton, *The Presidents and Civil Disorder*, Washington, D.C.: Brookings Institution, 1941.

Riker, William H., *Soldiers of the States: The Role of the National Guard in American Democracy*, Washington, D.C.: Public Affairs Press, 1957.

Root, Elihu, "Elihu Root to Lieutenant General S. B. M. Young, September 17, 1916," in Robert Bacon and James Brown Scott, eds., *The Military and Colonial Policy of the United States: Addresses and Reports*, New York: AMS Press, 1970.

Rosswurm, Steven J., *Arms, Country, and Class: The Philadelphia Militia and the Lower Sort During the American Revolution*, New Brunswick, N.J.: Rutgers University Press, 1989.

Rostker, Bernard, *I Want You! The Evolution of the All-Volunteer Force*, Santa Monica, Calif.: RAND Corporation, MG-265-RC, 2006. As of October 18, 2016:
http://www.rand.org/pubs/monographs/MG265.html

Royster, Charles, *A Revolutionary People at War: The Continental Army and American Character, 1775–1783*, Chapel Hill, N.C.: University of North Carolina Press, 1979.

Saltonstall, Leverett, *Status of Reserve and National Guard Forces of the Armed Services Report of the Interim Subcommittee on Preparedness of the Committee on Armed Services*, Washington, D.C.: Chairman of the Senate Committee on Armed Services, January 29, 1954.

Schlesinger, J. R., and U.S. Department of Defense Historical Office, *Public Statements of James R. Schlesinger, Secretary of Defense*, Washington, D.C., 1973.

Scott, James Brown, *The Militia: Extracts from the Journals and Debates of the Federal Convention, the State Constitutional Conventions, the Congress, the Federalist, Together with Papers Relating to the Militia of the United States*, 64th Congress, 2d Session, Senate, Document No. 695, January 12, 1917

The Second Constitution of the State of New York, Article II, Section 2, 1821.

Secretary of War and the Bureau Chiefs, *Annual Report of the War Department, 1902*, Vol. 2, Washington, D.C.: U.S. House of Representatives, 1903.

Shannon, Fred A., *The Organization and Administration of the Union Army*, Bethesda, Md.: University Publications of America, 1994.

Shaw, William L., *The Civil War Federal Conscription and Exemption System*, Washington, D.C.: Judge Advocates Association, 1962a.

———, "The Confederate Conscription and Exemption Acts," *American Journal of Legal History*, Vol. 6, No. 4, October, 1962b, pp. 368–405.

———, "The Interrelationship of the United States Army and the National Guard," *Military Law Review*, No. 39, January 1966, pp. 39–84.

Shy, John, "A New Look at the Colonial Militia," *William and Mary Quarterly*, Vol. 3, No. 20, 1963.

———, *A People Numerous and Armed: Reflections on the Military Struggle for American Independence*, Oxford, UK: Oxford University Press, 1976.

Singer, P. W., *The Rise of the Privatized Military Industry*, updated ed., Ithaca, N.Y.: Cornell University Press, 2007.

Skelton, William B., *The United States Army, 1821–1837: An Institutional History*, PhD dissertation, Evanston, Ill.: Northwestern University, 1968.

———, *An American Profession of Arms: The Army Officer Corps, 1784–1861*, Lawrence, Kan.: University Press of Kansas, 1992.

Smith, Jonathan, "How Massachusetts Raised Her Troops in the American Revolution," *Massachusetts Historical Society*, 1922.

Spiller, Roger, "Calhoun's Expansible Army: The History of a Military Idea," *South Atlantic Quarterly*, Spring 1980.

Stanley, Bruce, *Outsourcing Security: Private Military Contractors and U.S. Foreign Policy*, Potomac, Md.: Potomac Books, 2015.

Steuben, F. W. von, "A Letter on the Subject of an Established Militia," New York, 1784.

Stimson, Henry L., *What Is the Matter with Our Army?* Washington, D.C.: U.S. Government Printing Office, 1912.

Stueck, William Whitney, *Rethinking the Korean War: A New Diplomatic and Strategic History*, Princeton, N.J.: Princeton University Press, 2002.

Thomas, T. H., "*The Biography of the Late Marshal Foch*, by Major-General Sir George Aston," *American Historical Review*, Vol. 35, No. 4, July 1930, pp. 613–615.

Todd, Frederick P., "Our National Guard: An Introduction to Its History," published in two parts in *Military Affairs*, Vol. 5, No. 2, Summer 1941a, and Vol. 5, No. 3, Autumn 1941b.

Upton, Emory, *The Armies of Asia and Europe: Embracing Official Reports on the Armies of Japan, China, India, Persia, Italy, Russia, Austria, Germany, France, and England, Accompanied by Letters Descriptive of a Journey from Japan to the Caucasus*, New York: Appleton, 1878.

———, *The Military Policy of the United States*, 4 ed., Washington, D.C.: U.S. Government Printing Office, (1903) 1917.

U.S. Code, Title 10, Subtitle B, Section 3062(c), Policy; Composition; Organized Peace Establishment, 2012.

U.S. Code, Title 32, National Guard, 2012.

U.S. General Staff, *Statement of Proper Military Policy for the United States*, Washington, D.C.: U.S. Government Printing Office, 1916.

U.S. House of Representatives, *Officers' Reserve Corps—National Guard (Proposed Amendments to the National Defense Act, H.R. 10478: Hearings Before the Committee on Military Affairs)*, Washington, D.C.: U.S. Government Printing Office, 1930.

———, *Review of the Reserve Program: Hearing Before the Subcommittee No. 1 of the Committee on Armed Services*, Washington, D.C.: U.S. Government Printing Office, February 4–8, 18–21, 1957.

———, *Hearings on Proposed Merger of Army Reserve Components: Hearing Before the Subcommittee No. 2 of the Committee on Armed Services*, Washington, D.C.: U.S. Government Printing Office, March 25, 1965.

U.S. House of Representatives, Committee on Military Affairs, *National Guard Bill*, House Report 141, 73rd Congress, 1st Session, Washington, D.C.: U.S. Government Printing Office, 1933.

U.S. Senate, *Testimony of Assistant Secretary of Defense William Brehm on Defense, Manpower, and Reserve Affairs: Hearing Before the Committee on Armed Service, Subcommittee on Manpower and Personnel*, Washington, D.C.: U.S. Government Printing Office, July 30, 1975.

U.S. Senate, Committee on Military Affairs, *Amend the National Defense Act*, Senate Report 135, 73rd Congress, 1st Session, Washington, D.C.: U.S. Government Printing Office, 1933.

U.S. Statutes at Large, An Act to Provide for Calling Forth the Militia to Execute the Laws of the Union, Suppress Insurrections and Repel Invasions, Second Congress, Session I, Chapter 28, May 2, 1792 (1 Stat. 264).

U.S. Statutes at Large, An Act to More Effectually to Provide for the National Defense by Establishing a Uniform Militia Throughout the United States, Second Congress, Session I, Chapter 33, May 8, 1792 (1 Stat. 271).

U.S. Statutes at Large, An Act Authorizing the Employment of the Land and Naval Forces of the United States, in Case of Insurrections, Tenth Congress, Session II, Chapter 39, March 8, 1807 (2 Stat. 443).

U.S. Statutes at Large, An Act to Provide for the Suppression of Rebellion Against and Resistance to the Laws of the United States, and to Amend the Act Entitled "An Act to Provide for Calling Forth the Militia to Execute the Laws of the Union" Passed February Twenty-Eight, Seventeen Hundred and Ninety-Five, 37th Congress, 1st Session, Chapter 25, July 29, 1861 (12 Stat. 281).

U.S. Statutes at Large, An Act to Amend the Act Calling Forth the Militia to Execute the Laws of the Union, Suppress Insurrections, and Repel Invasions, Approved February Twenty-Eight, Seventeen Hundred and Ninety-Five, and the Acts Amendatory Thereof, and for Other Purposes, Thirty-Seventh Congress, Session II, Chapter 201, July 17, 1862 (12 Stat. 597).

U.S. Statutes at Large, An Act for Enrolling and Calling Out the National Forces, and for Other Purposes, Thirty-Seventh Congress, Session III, Chapter 75, March 3, 1863 (12 Stat. 781).

U.S. Statutes at Large, An Act to Provide for Temporarily Increasing the Military Establishment of the United States in Time of War, and for Other Purposes, Fifty-Fifth Congress, Session II, Chapter 187, April 22, 1898 (30 Stat. 361).

U.S. Statutes at Large, An Act to Increase the Efficiency of the Permanent Military Establishment of the United States, Fifty-Sixth Congress, Session II, Chapter 192, February 2, 1901 (31 Stat. 748).

U.S. Statutes at Large, An Act to Promote the Efficiency of the Militia, and for Other Purposes, Fifty-Seventh Congress, Session II, Chapter 196, January 21, 1903 (32 Stat. 775).

U.S. Statutes at Large, An Act to Increase the Efficiency of the Medical Department of the United States Army, Sixtieth Congress, Session I, Chapter 150, April 23, 1908 (35 Stat. 66).

U.S. Statutes at Large, An Act to Further Amend the Act Entitled "An Act to Promote the Efficiency of the Militia and for Other Purposes, Approved January Twenty-First Nineteen Hundred and Three," Sixteenth Congress, Session I, Chapter 204, May 27, 1908 (35 Stat. 399).

U.S. Statutes at Large, An Act to Authorize the President to Increase Temporarily the Military Establishment of the United States, Sixty-Fifth Congress, Session 1, Chapter 15, May 18, 1917 (40 Stat. 76).

Uviller, H. Richard, and William G. Merkel, "The Second Amendment in Context: The Case of the Vanishing Predicate," *Chicago-Kent Law Review*, Vol. 76, January 2000.

———, *The Militia and the Right to Arms, or, How the Second Amendment Fell Silent*, Durham, N.C.: Duke University Press, 2002.

Vladeck, Stephen I., "The Field Theory: Martial Law, the Suspension Power, and the Insurrection Act," *Temple Law Review*, Vol. 80, No. 2, 2007, pp. 391–440.

———, "The Calling Forth Clause and the Domestic Commander in Chief," *Cardozo Law Review*, Vol. 29, No. 3, 2008, pp. 1091–1108.

———, "Emergency Power and the Militia Acts," *The Yale Law Journal*, Vol. 114, No. 1, October 2004.

———, *The Calling Forth Clause and the Domestic Commander In-Chief*, Research Paper, Washington, D.C.: American University Washington College of Law, 2008.

Volunteers of America, *Proceedings of the Convention of National Guards*, St. Louis, Mo., October 1, 1879.

Walsh, Ellard A., "Ellard Walsh to the Adjutants Generals of the Several States and the Territories and Members of the Executive Committee of the National Guard Conference," *Universal Military Training*, February 19, 1944.

———, "Address to the Army War College (February 1953)," in Ellard A. Walsh and Edgar C. Erickson, *The Nation's National Guard*, Washington, D.C.: National Guard Association of the United States, 1954.

War Department, *Reduction of the Army*, Washington, D.C.: 16th Congress, Second Session, 1820.

Ward, Matthew C., "The American Militias: 'The Garnish of the Table'?" in Roger Chickering and Stig Förster, eds., *War in an Age of Revolution, 1775–1815*, Cambridge, UK: Cambridge University Press, 2010.

Warren, Jason W., *Connecticut Unscathed: Victory in the Great Narragansett War, 1675–1676*, Norman, Okla.: University of Oklahoma Press, 2014.

Washington, George, "Letter to Baron von Steuben," Mount Vernon, March 15, 1784.

———, "Sentiments on a Peace Establishment, 1783," in Dethloff, Henry C. and Gerald E. Shenk, eds., *Citizen and Soldier: A Sourcebook on Military Service and National Defense from Colonial America to the Present*, New York and London: Routledge, (1783) 2011.

Watson, Samuel J., *Jackson's Sword: The Army Officer Corps on the American Frontier, 1810–1821*, Lawrence, Kan.: University Press of Kansas, 2012.

———, *Peacekeepers and Conquerors: The Army Officer Corps on the American Frontier, 1821–1846*, Lawrence, Kan.: Kansas University Press, 2013.

Weigley, Russell Frank, *Towards an American Army: Military Thought from Washington to Marshall*, New York: Columbia University Press, 1962.

———, *History of the United States Army*, New York: Macmillan, 1967.

———, *The American Way of War: A History of United States Military Strategy and Policy*, New York: Macmillan, 1973.

Wiener, Frederick Bernays, "The Militia Clause of the Constitution," *Harvard Law Review*, Vol. 54, No. 2, 1940, pp. 181–220.

Wilson, Frederick T., *Federal Aid in Domestic Disturbances, 1787–1903*, New York: Arno Press, 1969.

Wilson, Frederick T., and U.S. Adjutant-General's Office, *Federal Aid in Domestic Disturbances, 1787–1903*, Washington, D.C.: U.S. Government Printing Office, 1903.

Winthrop, William, *Military Law and Precedents*, Boston: Little, Brown, and Company, 1896.

Wood, Gordon S., *The Creation of the American Republic, 1776–1787*, Chapel Hill, N.C.: University of North Carolina Press, 1998.

Wood, Leonard, *The Military Obligation of Citizenship*, Princeton, N.J.: Princeton University Press, 1915.

Woodward, C. Vann, "The Age of Reinterpretation," *American Historical Review*, Vol. 66, No. 1, October 1960.

Zelner, Kyle F., *A Rabble in Arms: Massachusetts Towns and Militiamen During King Philip's War*, New York: New York University Press, 2010.